GRANDPA'S WAR:

THE FRENCH ADVENTURES OF A WORLD WAR I AMBULANCE DRIVER

By Edward Greeman

Writers and Readers Publishing, Inc.

WRITERS AND READERS PUBLISHING, INCORPORATED
P.O. Box 461, Village Station
New York, NY 10014

c/o Airlift Book Company
26 Eden Grove
London N7 8EF
England

Copyright © 1992
Library of Congress Catalog Card Number
ISBN # 0-86316-098-0
1 2 3 4 5 6 7 8 9 0

Manufactured in the United States of America

TABLE OF CONTENTS

EDITOR'S FOREWORD

BY RICHARD GREEMAN

As a boy, I always loved listening to my Dad's World War I stories, and it is with great pleasure that I pass them on to you — written down here for the first time.

Dad originally penned these stories in the form of letters to me — written between his 75th and 93rd birthdays. I eventually collected them and arranged them in logical order for his grandchildren — hence the title, *Grandpa's War*. Together, they form an engaging memoir of the young years of an American who was born with this century as well as a highly personal — and fascinating — historical perspective on the "Great War" of 1914-1918 and related events. Paul Fussell, the author of *The Great War and Modern Memory*, read them "with interest and admiration" and praised Dad's "pretty wit and laudable humanity."

Among these pages a lost world comes vividly to life — and turns out to be not so different from out own. What *is* different are the eyes through which it is viewed. Teddy Greeman's had seen all of seventeen summers when he landed in France in 1917, and his youth was that of the American Century. We have learned a great deal about ourselves since then — much of it painful. Dad's stories manage to reflect that painful knowledge while at the same time vividly recreating the easy innocence, boundless optimism, and unfailing good humor of then.

One historical note: In 1917, writers like Ernest Hemingway, John Dos Passos and e.e. cummings, who formed the first wave of World War I volunteer ambulance drivers, said their "farewell to arms." These generally older and wealthier volunteers had to resign from the privately-organized American

Field Service when the American Expeditionary Force entered the conflict. They were replaced by young men like seventeen-year-old Edward "Teddy" Greeman from N.Y.U., who served in the United States Army Ambulance Corps through to the end of the war. Dad's memoirs thus deal with a later period and a much more plebeian service than those of his literary predecessors. Moreover, "Grandpa" Teddy had also outlived them all when he got around to writing up his own *French Adventures of a World War I Ambulance Driver.*

This Jewish Boy Scout from Westchester County, New York, lived to serve his country again in yet a Second World War. And in 1968, he found himself marching again — down Fifth Avenue with the Vietnam Veterans Against War — in order to prevent a Third one.

Rich in history, *Grandpa's War* is above all a wise and charming tale by an amazing old man. Enjoy it.

WEST HARTFORD, CONNECTICUT
JUNE, 1992

DEDICATION

I have come a long way from the USAAC to the VFP — that is, from the United States Army Ambulance Corps of 1917 to the Veterans For Peace of 1992. But maybe my transition is not such a strange one. We World War I ambulance drivers, although patriotic, were dedicated to bringing aid and succor to the wounded — of both armies. Veterans For Peace is dedicated to eliminating the need for future USAACs.

We were not fire eaters in that far away peacetime of 1916 when our President, Woodrow Wilson, was reelected on the slogan "He Kept Us Out Of War." And in 1917, when Wilson broke his promise, and we sailed for France, our cartridge belts were filled not with bullets but with iodine swabs. Our aggressiveness was limited to threatening to "Hock the Kaiser" — a pun on the German war cry "*Hoch der Kaiser*" ("Up with the Kaiser!") — by putting iodine on German wounds until they cried for peace.

And when, only yesterday, another President, Mr. Bush, waged war for nebulous reasons in the Persian Gulf, many Americans, in and out of uniform, could not understand why. Looking backward, we were not so different. The French have a phrase for it: "*Plus ça change, plus ça la même chose.*" — "The more things change, the more they stay the same."

I dedicate my memoirs of World War I to Veterans For Peace and to all Americans actively dedicated to preventing another senseless war. They represent the strongest barrier against it.

EDWARD "TEDDY" GREEMAN,
UNITED STATES ARMY AMBULANCE CORPS

PHOTOGRAPHS

CHAPTER I

HOW TO LOSE AN AMBULANCE

I suppose my reminiscences should begin with a modicum of violence. After all, it was a "World War." So I will recount how I lost an ambulance to enemy shell fire.

It all begins with the history of the *briquet* or cigarette lighter.

To understand this essential wartime invention, you must know that there was a shortage of matches and more than enough smokers of cigarettes, both tailor-made and hand-rolled — plus pipes that required constant relighting. Also, most of the matches available were sulphur-tipped — which required a special technique. You had to light the match and hold it away from the cigarette until the evil-smelling, horrible-tasting sulphur was burned off. Then you could light up. But by that time, if there was any wind blowing, the match was out. So necessity, ever the mother of invention, produced the *briquet*.

The base of the *briquet* was made of a machine-gun shell casing. This is a brass cylinder about an inch in diameter and three inches long, one of which is ejected onto the ground every time a shot is fired — that is to say, several times a second. The empty casing can be stuffed with absorbent cotton — stolen from first aid dressings — and a flint and steel is attached to the top. Now when filled with gasoline you have a useful object — a practical lighter. Every *poilu* — the French version of our "G.I." (the word actually means "hairy guy") — had one, and so did a lot of Englishmen, Italians, Portuguese, Indochinese, Madagascans, Algerians and a few assorted soldiers without credentials.

I have accounted for the source of the shell and the stuffing, but where to get the gasoline? Very simple. Every ambulance had two 5-liter cans strapped to the running boards as spares in case the tank should go dry. Actually, the gas tank itself could be emptied by siphoning — but this required a long rubber tube and a lot of time during which the thief could be apprehended. The spare cans were easier to rob. The straps were plain leather with a buckle, no lock and key, and you helped yourself while the driver was sleeping in his dugout or even in the cab. This situation had spread to such an extent that most drivers checked to see if the cans were full or empty before going on a run. But that didn't work either, as you will see.

Going from this general discussion to my particular involvement, we come to the Second Battle of the Marne. History, so fond of repeating itself, had placed the opposing armies, after nearly four years of war (from "The Guns of August," 1914, to Bastille Day, July 14, 1918) almost exactly in the same positions. In '14, the German cavalry got to Meaux on the Marne, fourteen kilometers from Paris. (They were stopped there by the French Army, brought hurriedly from Paris, by the famous "Taxicabs of the Marne.") In '18 it was Château-Thierry, about ten kilometers further east. That story is well known, as this was the first major involvement of the American Expeditionary Force (the famous "A.E.F.").

Our division, the French XVII, to which we American ambulance drivers of SSU 592 were attached, was on the other side of the bulge which the advancing German armies had created. We worked out of Epernay, also on the Marne, and, eventually, our troops working west and others working east squeezed the Germans out of the bulge, and they had to retreat to the north — back where they started from. It was really the beginning of the end, but it didn't look like it as the Jerries (our affectionate term for the enemy) had plenty of clout left, and if they retreated, it was no rout.

We had our usual set up — four of our ambulances at the Front, each at a first aid post of one regiment, four more, half way back, to act as relief, and then four more at the base, to move up as the first lot came in loaded. I was in the first lot on July 20th, 1918, as the pressure was being applied to force the Germans north.

I had slept the night (quite well, thank you) in a ruined house in Fleury-La-Rivière, and in the morning I got a load of four *assis* — seated wounded. They had been gassed and wore bandages over their eyes. I started off. It was a lovely, sunny morning, and we were now a good three miles back of the fighting. So it was relatively quiet. The road wound up hill in the traditional fashion — a slow climb east for a quarter of a mile or so, then a hairpin turn and repeat west — eventually reaching the top of the Montagne de Rheims. Yes, it's the same place where they have the Cathedral and the champagnes.

About half way up I ran out of gas, but I wasn't worried. I just got out and unstrapped my cans, which were full, and dumped the contents into the tank. Then I twirled the crank a few times, but nothing happened. So I took the wooden stick with which we measured the gas in the tank and dipped and smelled and tasted and knew at once that my tank was full of water. The *briquet* fillers had screwed me good. They had stolen the gas and filled the cans with water!

I was annoyed — in fact, I was furious — but not worried. I got my wounded out and told them to form a line, each with a hand on the next man's shoulders. I pointed them in the right direction and said "Go," in excellent French. "At the top of this hill, only 500 meters away, is a fine, upstanding American named Alan Richard Kelly, familiarly known as 'Bon Dick.' He will take you to the hospital and dispatch a tow truck to get me out of here and peace be with you."

But they weren't having any. "You signed for us," they retorted, with the Frenchman's insistence on bureaucratic protocol. "And you must stay with us until you turn us in at the hospital and get a receipt."

Of course they were correct. So I abandoned my chariot — a court-martial offense — and started up the hill with my wounded. A few seconds later, we flattened as we heard a shell coming

My blown-up buggy. July 1918.

in — I know you don't hear the one that hits you, but you duck just the same.

Then there was quiet, and we continued. But when we rounded the next curve and looked back, my beautiful rig was no more. Some Kraut gunner had spotted this motionless green truck with a large red cross on a circular white ground painted on its side. The target was too tempting. Without bracketing shots, he let one go and got a bull's eye. It was a high explosive shell that exploded on contact — there was no big hole in the road. It must have just lifted the body off the chassis and thrown it a few feet away and cut the I-beams in half. My blouse (the military term for jacket) and the klaxon horn it threw into a tree nearby — and the rest was little tiny pieces, scattered in the road.

By an enormous coincidence, a friend of mine came by just then. He was the Protestant *Aumônier* (chaplain) of the division. And he had a camera — so the result is preserved for posterity.

By that time Kelly, in the other car, had come down to meet us, and he took our men into the H.O.E. (Hospital of Evacuation), and I got a replacement car and a new blouse. There is no moral to this tale. French intransigence had saved my life — I had planned to snatch a little shut-eye in the wagon while waiting for the tow truck. Also the "Dutchmen" (slang for "*Deutsch* ") had confirmed their fondness for using the red cross as a target — this was not news to anybody.

As to what our side did, I have no statistics, but, some months later, we did capture whole German field hospitals intact. And they did not have holes in the ground where the big red cross was outlined in white-washed pebbles, as ours did.

Well, maybe we were younger then, and Vietnam wasn't even in the dictionary.

And now, I ask you — how did a nice, Jewish boy from Larchmont, New York, get into a mess like this?

Thereby hangs a tale . . .

CHAPTER II

FROM CRACOW TO ST. NAZAIRE

You would not understand how I came to enlist in the United States Army Medical Corps in 1917, at the age of seventeen, unless you knew that I had been in Plattsburg, New York, in the Citizens Volunteer Training Corps, a year earlier. And you certainly would not understand what I was doing there, at the age of sixteen, unless you knew that my father was there, too, at age 39 — or maybe 40. That involves knowing more about my father, Louis Greeman, and you could go all the way back to Adam and Eve if you really wanted to know what makes me tick. But I think it would be enough to start with Aaron, my grandfather, especially as we don't know anything about his forebears.

You notice I said "Aaron" and didn't add the "Greeman." That was deliberate. My grandfather was born in Cracow, at that time part of the Austro-Hungarian Empire, about 1845, as nearly as I can figure out. Cracow, as my father was fond of pointing out, was a famous university town, the site of one of the oldest institutions of learning on the Continent, but it is of little consequence to our personal history. For one thing, Aaron was a little Jewish boy — and Jewish boys did not go to the University of Cracow, and secondly, his father and mother died of the plague — or some perennial epidemic (cholera or typhus, maybe) — when he was six, and a few years later he was brought to the United States by an uncle.

This uncle's name, or the name he took, was Nussbaum, and his descendants bear it to this day.

My grandfather Aaron settled in New York, became an American citizen in the 1860s and someone — possibly a clerk in a government office — wrote down his name as "Greeman." To the best of my knowledge, and I have looked all over, there are no other Greemans — plenty of "Greenmans" — but as to our name we are unique. It is a great nuisance because our mail goes astray, and we can hardly ever get phone messages correctly. Of course, that also applies to people named "Smith" so it is nothing to worry about.

Aaron's uncle Nussbaum settled in St. Louis, and he even had a concession, a beer garden and restaurant, at the St. Louis World's Fair of 1904 (about which Judy Garland sang the trolley song in "*Meet Me In St. Louis*"). In fact, "I vas dere, Charley," at the tender age of four — which is interesting because it reflects on my father's philosophy, of which more anon.

My grandfather, Aaron Greeman.

Aaron Greeman married a hometown girl from Cracow and raised a family in the New York ghetto. He and his wife had ten children, of whom only four survived infancy. The graves of six children, aged one to four, could be found — at least when I was a child — in one of those cemeteries in Brooklyn where most of that generation were laid to rest. Infant mortality was common and widespread in the 1870s in New York, particularly in the Jewish ghetto — which does not need explaining. The conditions are well known. My father, Louis, survived — but he was a skinny, undernourished kid who grew up bow-legged, he always claimed, because of malnutrition. Partly this was due to poverty and partly to the diet which was followed by Jewish people attempting to keep a kosher house.

My father was not anti-Semitic — but he was close to it — and he claimed, with a good deal of common sense, that the matzoth balls of Jewish home cooking had killed more Jews than cannon balls. It is certain that they didn't have green vegetables, or, if they were there, they didn't eat them.

The four young Greemans who survived all lived to a fairly advanced age and were reasonably healthy. My father was the only one who was bow-legged — although his three sisters might all have been as far as anyone could tell. They all wore three petticoats and a skirt, especially the one who became a schoolteacher. The old man, Aaron, developed a home industry — he made bow ties in the kitchen-dining room-living room of their cold water flat. I guess everybody in the family tied bows and stuck them on cards. Apparently it paid well enough so that the three girls and my father got through the eighth grade — and at least one girl to high school and normal school.

My father worked after school for E.A. Ridley, a department store, when he was eleven. He was a cash boy, running between the counter and the cashier's desk to make change. His job was later rendered obsolete by the cash register and an ingenious system of little boxes that darted around the ceilings in the big stores on a system of wires and springs — a delightful sight for small fry to watch, in my childhood.

By the time he was sixteen, my father had a full-time job with L. Strauss & Sons. This was the family that in its next generation saw the rise of several merchant princes — philanthropists, ambassadors, etc. These were the Strausses of Macy's (one of whom, with his wife, went down on the *Titanic*), and it was their father that my father worked for.

But when he was twenty, Louis took the first steps that made him "different" and to which I am now, at long last, coming. He had been to night school, had joined the Emma Lazarus Society (she wrote the words on the Statue of Liberty), had fallen in love and gotten married — all this following the pattern of many of his contemporaries.

But now he applied for a job with a firm that advertised "No Jews Need Apply." I am not certain at this late date whether those words were used — but it was certainly not uncommon, and if they used a euphemism, it was unmistakable. Even twenty years later (around 1915), the papers carried ads that said "Christian Boy Wanted."

But Louis didn't "look Jewish," and he had a fine gift of the gab — and, what's more, he took his father with him. The "old man" — Aaron must have been fifty — had a close-cropped mustache and a frock coat, probably rented, and he looked like Grover Cleveland — I have the picture to prove it (see page 16) — and Louis got the job — with A.A. Vantine & Co.

The name is Dutch. The original Vantine was a Hollander and a ship's captain who entered Japan not long after Admiral Perry. Subsequently, he dropped anchor in New York harbor and opened a wholesale and retail establishment for the sale of Japanese goods — silk, porcelain, and all the other products of original and indigenous Oriental artists. It was enormously successful and fitted in with the taste of the day — late Victorian.

So my daddy was launched on a successful career just about the same time that I appeared — that is, 1899.

All the other employees were Christians, and we appear to have moved into a Christian neighborhood about that time. Certainly, I grew up with absolutely no realization that I was any different from my contemporaries. We lived in a succession of boarding houses and later apartments — in odd places. Not of course in the ghetto from whence my old man had come, but not either in the new ghetto — Harlem (not Black at that time) or Washington Heights where my aunts and uncles lived.

We even lived for awhile in half of a private house on Henderson Place, in Yorkville, where the signs said "*Zahnarzt*" instead of "Dentist." This was okay with me. I knew a lot of German at age six because my mother was a German Jew named Reba Meyer — and that was my father's other unusual step because Russian Jews or Polish Jews didn't marry German Jews. Actually, the prejudices were almost as strong as those against intermarriage with Gentiles. Nobody even mentioned "miscegenation" — nobody knew what it meant.

When I was nine and had a baby sister, we moved to Mamaroneck, New York, which is in Westchester County, and that must have been a bombshell to both the families — my father's and my mother's. My mother still had five sisters and my father three — all with families, my cousins, living between 110th Street and 181st Street in Manhattan. And they thought my crazy father was taking their sister and her innocent children to Siberia.

It wasn't that bad. In fact, the New Haven Railroad in those days was more dependable than it was ninety years later. But it was still "the country" and that is in quotes. The Mamaroneck River flowed past the little residential park in which we lived — it was called Harbor Heights because you could see the harbor if you climbed to the top of the highest tree around. You could still trap muskrat two blocks from your door, and the Big Woods (Saxons Woods) was two miles away. Later, as a Boy Scout, I camped overnight on what became the golf course.

Again, there were no Jews, or only a very few, in the community. There was no synagogue in Mamaroneck until many years later so my religious ties were nonexistent. I stress this point because my father was such a 100% flag-waving American that I naturally followed in his footsteps — and there was no other force suggesting any alternative in our daily lives.

Now we get to 1912 and a "first" in contemporary history — a break in the ranks of the major political parties. Theodore Roosevelt founded the Progressive or "Bull Moose" party. My father had been a Roosevelt worshipper since the time of San Juan Hill. I was named Edward, after a friend of the family, and one of my father's best customers was one Edward M. Sibley. Mr. Sibley was English and as was, and still is, the English custom, his nick-name was "Teddy." This fitted perfectly into my father's plans — I became Edward "Teddy" Greeman and have remained so to this day. Parenthetically, the same people who cannot get my surname correctly over the phone are completely baffled when they try to decide on my first name.

My sister was named "Theodora." She too had a godfather, one of my father's poker-playing pals — Theodore Prince. He was a bachelor at the time, and wealthy, and my father had an idea he might be generous to his god-daughter. (He never was.) But, on top of that, Theodore Roosevelt by that time was President of the United States. Much later, a friend of mine, learning of our names, offered a classic remark in our family's history, "If Edward is called 'Teddy,' I assume that Theodora is called 'Edwina.'"

The following was typical of my father. In April of 1912, the *Titanic* sank under circumstances that caused a great deal of uproar — she went too far north, she went too fast, there were not enough lifeboats, etc.

What few people recall is that the *Titanic* had a sister ship, the *Olympic* — two years older and about ten feet shorter. She had been the wonder of the world until the *Titanic* was launched. Now she was a white elephant. So the White Star Line cut the prices on her staterooms by about 50%, and my old man bought round trips to London and Paris — long before such things were common, except for Morgans and Rockefellers. He took my mother, my sister and myself. Theo was five and traveled free. I was twelve and half fare — so the whole deal for the family was easy for a man making $100 a week (no income tax).

It was not all beer and skittles — I did a lot of baby-sitting and would probably have been happier playing with boys and girls of my own age — but it is typical of my father, who couldn't withstand a bargain and couldn't imagine that anyone, young or old, would rather be any other place than with him.

The cream of the jest was that on the first day out we had life boat drill — then just instituted — and were issued life belts that said "R.M.S. Titanic" very lightly painted over and changed to "R.M.S. Olympic."

It was just two months after the tragedy.

Now back to the original "Teddy." He lost the election of 1912 but split the Republican Party and elected Woodrow Wilson. Mr. Wilson received 6 million votes, Roosevelt 4 million and William Howard Taft 3 million, so there is no doubt how the "old schoolmaster" became President just as Europe was about to burst into flames.

Just two years later, the "Guns of August,"1914, marked the outbreak of what would go down in history as "World War <u>ONE</u>" — although we didn't know it at the time. What we did know was that our President and his Secretary of State, William Jennings Bryan, were strictly neutral and said so at every opportunity.

Meanwhile, Teddy Roosevelt, who had been in involuntary retirement, emerged to fight for a cause — "Preparedness." Along with General Leonard Wood, a buddy of his from the Cuban campaign, he preached his message at every opportunity — and he convinced the government to permit concerned citizens to go to a regular Army post (in Plattsburg, New York) at their own expense and pay for six weeks training as infantrymen.

My father, Louis Greeman, at Plattsburg, 1916.

To appreciate this situation you must remember that Irving Berlin had just written an enormously popular song, "I Didn't Raise My Boy to Be a Soldier."

Two years later he was writing, "Oh! How I Hate to Get up in the Morning." But, in 1916, while Wilson was running for reelection on the slogan "He Kept Us Out Of War," there were men leaving daily for Canada to enlist, and the American Field Service and the Lafayette Escadrille were more and more on everyone's mind.

This was the perfect setting for my father. He was nearly

forty. I was nearly sixteen. There were two sections of volunteer trainees — senior and junior. He was really too old for the former — I was a trifle too young for the latter. So we both went. Papa paid for both of us, although we later got our money back, and the snapshots in my album show him, bow-legged, wearing thick glasses and a hearing aid, carrying a 30-30 Springfield rifle and bravely doing squads east and west. Pop didn't quite make it — he gave up after four weeks by mutual agreement — but I stuck it out and enjoyed it. In fact it was a bright spot in my life.

Because of my precocity — I was born with a good memory — I went through school at a rapid pace. In those days you could "skip" if it seemed logical to the school authorities. So I graduated from grammar school at twelve having done eight grades in four years — and that meant I was out of high school a few days before my sixteenth birthday.

This had a ruinous effect on my personal life. I was always in classrooms full of older and bigger boys and girls — while my physical playmates were several classes behind me. I couldn't play with them — and my classmates wouldn't "play" with me. I was also overweight and had poor co-ordination, so baseball, football, etc., were only something to read about. When players were chosen for any sport involving teams, I was picked last — and then only if I was needed to fill a gap. I did do well in the Boy Scouts. I could walk — I had good feet — and I could excel in the part of scouting that involved a good memory. This all stood me in good stead at Plattsburg.

Best of all, in Plattsburg I learned I could discharge a rifle and come close to hitting a target. This was a great surprise as I had, up to that time, been afraid of firecrackers on the Fourth of July. This is a profound experience for someone who has never won a fist fight. As the gangsters say, a gun is a great equalizer. Suddenly I was the equal of the other men in my squad — all

My platoon in Plattsburg, 1916. I am at the lower right.

WASPs and all good at sports.

My proudest moment came by chance on our 90-mile hike — which climaxed the six weeks of training. At about 5 p.m., we had just put up our pup tents — we slept on the ground. A bevy of generals, headed by General Leonard Wood himself, came to review the troops. They stopped at intervals, and I happened to be one of the stops. "How are your feet?" General Wood asked me, and when I replied that I was feeling no pain, he asked me how I accounted for that, and I told him that I had been a Boy Scout. Instead of provoking a big laugh, he turned to his colleagues and said, "The Boy Scouts have done our country a good turn — our boys can march with the best of them."

The cream of that particular jest is that two years later the American Expeditionary Force was almost completely motorized and the "Big Parade" of the A.E.F. was a fleet of trucks going up the "Via Sacre," a road left over from the defense of Verdun in 1916. But Plattsburg had made a tin soldier out of "Teddy."

Plattsburg has some interesting asides. Our Captain, a regular Army officer, advised us that our next armed conflict would be to put down the Negro uprising that he prophesied was coming. Also, I was the only Jew in our squad, and for one time in my life, I lied about it. I said I was pledged to Zeta PSI, a Gentile fraternity, and for six weeks I was regaled with jokes about Kikes and Sheenies. No, I did not defend myself, but I learned a lot about the "good old U.S. of A..," as Archie Bunker called it much later.

It didn't last long. In later years I marched again — but it was for "peace" and not war. In fact, my militarism lasted about a year — just long enough to get me into the Army — albeit as a non-combatant.

And the only other shooting I ever did was in the backyard of our billet in Nancy — in January of 1918 — when we lined up helmets of various issues — French, German, English and American — and shot at them with small arms — Lugers, Mausers and the like which we had obtained by slightly illicit means. The contest always came out the same way — the German helmet was the best, which strengthened our belief that we were on the wrong side.

This was best expressed by one John X. Bacso, who claimed to have a first cousin in the Austrian Army. Whenever he had his load on — which was often — he would climb on a table and declaim — "They've got beer in the German Army! Why the hell don't we have beer in our Army? *Hoch der Kaiser!*"

ABOUT THE BOY SCOUTS

In 1912, I had joined the B.S.A. (the Boy Scouts of America). This organization was founded, oddly enough, by an Englishman,

Sir Robert Baden-Powell, in 1908, and it is intriguing, in hindsight, that it was a pacifist movement that grew up a few years before World War I. Of course, at that time, we did not grasp the significance of the goals set forth by the founders — but it is obvious since we were equipped with wooden staves (plural of staff, I hope), whereas other boys had bb guns and played "soldier."

I was fortunate on two counts. Our first Scoutmaster was Edward Cave, editor of the *Boy Scout Magazine*, which gave Troop No. 1, Mamaroneck, New York, a certain kudos. His assistant, whose name escapes me, was the Rector of St. Thomas Church in Mamaroneck — a very ecumenical institution whose parish house was used for girl's basketball games and many other activities with no thought of racial, sexual or religious bigotry. (At this period, I scarcely knew I was a Jew. My mother found all the Jewish customs distasteful and hypocritical, which they were and are. For the most part, we ate ham, which the pious found sinful, but the Jewish doctors prescribed bacon bits for infants, which made them holy, in Reformed households.)

The second annual get-together, or Jamboree, of the B.S.A. was held in the Armory at 34th and Park Avenue, in New York City, which housed the 32nd Regiment of the National Guard. (The site now holds Norman Thomas High School.) We attended from far off Mamaroneck, twenty miles away, and saw plenty of guns. But the accent was on flora and fauna. There were awards for bird watching, wood crafts, hiking, etc. But no sharpshooter badges. It was not until four years later, when I went to Plattsburg to Civilian Military Training School and exchanged my staff for a gun, that I saw one of those.

Actually, I had no staff to turn in. A neighbor, Tommy Tibbets, had sawed it up in 12-inch lengths to play a child's form of baseball without a ball. You threw a short stick into the air and hit it with a longer one and ran bases. When I accused him of the theft he said, "Don't hit me." (I was a year older.) "I have confessed to the priest, and he gave me absolution."

I accepted his "confession," but I was out one Boy Scout staff.

CHAPTER III

FROM COLLEGE CAMPUS TO CAMP CRANE

*A*s I mull over in my mind the little stories, sad or funny, that I have been storing up since 1918, it seems to me that anyone who might some day read them would wonder how it all began — so here is a preface-type story.

In 1914 a great war broke out in Europe — it was to be known later as World War I. But its size and character were obvious from the start. Reams of paper have been covered explaining how it spread — particularly about how the United States became involved. I would like to comment on that. Our government was officially neutral — they made a big thing of being neutral in word and deed. Our future allies, England and France, primarily, borrowed money and bought arms here and encouraged those interested to tilt in their direction. But Germany had many friends here, too, and there was a powerful bloc that was Pro-German.

This is all history. Now let's take a "boy's eye view" of the situation. A young Jewish boy from the New York area, working his way through college — it could be City College or New York University (N.Y.U.) — looked on the war as a kind of blown-up Ivy League football game. He might favor Yale or Harvard, but it didn't affect him very deeply. Sure, there were volunteer ambulance drivers (and aviators) serving with the Allies — sons of wealthy parents whose outfit, the "Morgan-Harjes" units, carried the very names of the banking houses that were fueling the Allied machine. But as late as 1916, after two years of bitter fighting, it was possible to stage an enormous "German War Relief" spectacle in Madison Square Garden — and "I vas dere, Charley" and not alone. I was accompanied by a White Protestant American, one Charley Williams of Mamaroneck, New York, who, like many others, was "turned off" by England and France's ally — Czarist Russia, with its pogroms and a ruling family dominated by a mad monk named Rasputin who looked like John Barrymore with a beard. (In fact, he was — in the movie.)

We paid 25 cents to drive a nail (with "*Gott Mit Uns*" stamped on the head) into a wooden statue of Hindenburg (which may strike you as a strange way to express solidarity — the two bits notwithstanding). We ate good wurst and drank good beer — Prohibition was still three years away — and our young escort, one Otto Von Geissert, my father's assistant in the importing of Japanese novelties, was delighted to see these hundreds of German sympathizers.

Of course, the unusually inept German government changed that, even for Otto, in the next year.

Germany was being strangled by the Allied naval blockade and so "unrestricted" submarine warfare was begun, or restored, and after each sinking of a ship, usually carrying passengers of neutral nations, the Kaiser's ponderous propaganda mill would grind out the inevitable garbage — first, our submarines were nowhere near the scene of the disaster — second, the ship was full of munitions which exploded and sank in minutes leaving no survivors (*spurlos versenkt*) — and third, the commander of the submarine will be severely censured when he returns to port.

That kind of diet, in just about twelve months, turned the hard-working, studious boys of New York into volunteers to work alongside those sons-of-the-rich who were already working with the French Army in the American Field Service. And, in my own case, I was one of some thirty or forty at N.Y.U., on University Heights, who were in such a program in the winter of 1916.

Then, in April of 1917, war was declared and things started to happen. "Papa" Joffre came to the U.S. to beg for men to strengthen the French and British armies. He wanted soldiers in U.S. uniforms to be mixed into French or British divisions to shore up their morale. But we had a standing army of only 175,000, including officers. Obviously, every one of them was needed to act as an instructor for the much larger force that would be required and could not be sent over without months of training.

But there was a partial solution. According to U.S. law, the volunteers in the American Field Service ambulance corps could no longer serve a foreign government, even an ally, so they had to be replaced. And we had one thing that the Europeans didn't have — a large number of teenagers who could drive a car — thanks to Henry Ford and the "Tin Lizzie," the famous Model T Ford.

So a deal was made, and at N.Y.U. and a hundred other colleges the U.S.A.A.C. — that's the United States Army Ambulance Corps — was formed, to be sent over quickly so the Allies could see the uniform of the United States Army.

In our case, at N.Y.U., fate played a peculiar trick. The organizer of our unit happened to be one Chester F.S. Whitney, M.D. (the organizers were all M.D.s), who was the varsity doctor — the man with the black bag who ran out on the field when Fordham was too much for some N.Y.U. player. It was logical that he would head up our group, and upon our induction as an army unit he would be the Lieutenant. At this point, he learned — and we found out much later — that if he brought in 105 men, instead of 35, he would automatically become a Captain, as three units became a kind of battalion.

This appealed to the Doctor, who, incidentally, ended up as a Colonel with a beautiful suite at the Hotel Maurice in Paris — but he had a problem. The boys at N.Y.U. were either not interested in enlisting or were looking for more excitement than was

31

offered by driving an ambulance. (Now there were tanks, and Spads and our own submarines in the offing. A classmate of mine, Ted Cann, was the first man to receive the Congressional Medal of Honor in this war when he rescued the crew of a sub by his swimming prowess and courage.)

So Doc Whitney went to 14th Street and Broadway, Union Square, where on May 1st the labor unions staged their rallies, and for 364 other days a motley crew of panhandlers, drifters, derelicts and job hunters were prone to congregate. Here, too, was the biggest recruiting office for the Army and the Navy — they even had a plywood battleship to use as an office. Somehow, Doc got to a Sergeant with a sympathetic ear. He convinced him to send to N.Y.U. any man, preferably sober, who was just a little overweight, overage, flat footed or otherwise not quite up to Army standards. The doctor would then re-examine him and re-evaluate him on the green campus of University Heights far from the gray sidewalks of Manhattan.

For that is where they came from — and the end result was that Section 592 (my outfit) had the son of the president of the New York City subway system and a cab driver who had been involved with the escape of Harry K. Thaw (the assassin of the architect Stanford White) from Mattewan — the State Hospital for the Criminally Insane. Our roll call was a League of Nations in miniature. To the dozen or so students at the Heights (the original 35 were split up into three units), there were now added a short-order cook, a waiter, a bricklayer, a private chauffeur, an ex-movie actor and a camera man who had been with D.W. Griffith (he said) — all in all a colorful crew. But don't get me wrong, they were the greatest — and a much better source for stories with a punch than the typical All-American unit from Amherst or Harvard.

We did, however, present a slight disciplinary problem. Our average age was a lot higher than the other ambulance units, and these "men" — for that is what they were — had to be thoroughly mixed with the collegiate Rah-Rah Boys — which is what we were. And that's what this story is about.

Allentown, June 1917. No uniforms had been issued. I am in the second row, second from the right, facing the camera.

We were sworn into that man's army in May, 1917, and finally called out early in June. We reported to an armory and were taken to Allentown, Pennsylvania, where the fair grounds had been hastily transformed into a training camp. The race track oval was perfect for a drill field, and the track itself would have been great for ambulances — but we only had two cars for about 1500 men. The grandstand had a lot of open space underneath which was the logical mess hall — and the barracks were the horse stalls, cow byres, pig sties, etc., which a county fair grounds would naturally afford. This was not as bad as it sounds.

Everything had been whitewashed and fumigated — and the geography of the place was perfect for rugged individualists who were not used to a Sergeant at the door of the typical army barracks, bawling out the orders.

There was one drawback to the choice of location — the cesspools, which had never had so great a load over a prolonged period, couldn't take it. After a week, they overflowed. So some master mind organized a fleet of flat-bottom, three-ton Packard trucks — each equipped with twelve large, covered G.I. cans which were filled and hauled to a bottomless pit (probably an abandoned quarry) about three miles away.

There was one complication — the roads were rough. So each truck had to have a driver and twelve men — to sit, one apiece, on the cans, so the covers would not fall off and the contents spill over. At this point, we still had no uniforms. So I found myself fresh from the halls of academe, sitting on a large bucket of shit, in a dark-green, two-piece suit from Rogers Peet.

My neighbor, whose posterior was holding down the lid on the shit-can next to mine, was one Pete Algie, Peter Vincent Algie, to be exact, who was quickly christened "Coffee Pete" because he drank it constantly. He had a distinguishing feature — his nose had been flattened and was spread over his face. It fascinated me, and I must have been staring — so Pete told me his story.

"I see you are lookin' at my nose," he said, in the accent of the real New Yorker. "I got this right in my own neighborhood. There were a few of us standin' on the corner minding our own business. An' a cop comes by an says 'Move on!' an' we says 'Fuck you!' He goes away an' comes back after awhile an' says, 'I thought I tole youse guys to move,' an' we says, 'Fuck you!' — then he blows his whistle an' everywhere we look is cops wit' dizzy sticks an' dat's when I got dis nose. An' lemme tell you dis. You are younger dan me — an' I know my way aroun' — don' fight wit' no cops — remember dat — don't never fight wit' cops."

I have always remembered — to this day, I have never fought with a cop. But now you will understand how it could happen that one of our Privates, First Class, could wrestle in a manure heap with a First Lieutenant. And how we sent one "Looie" to the loony bin because he tried to make Boy Scouts out of us. But that was later.

July 1917 on leave from Allentown. With Catherine and Marguerite Thomas, my childhood sweetheart (she was 15).

P.S.

When I told you about "Coffee Pete" Algie — with the flattened nose — I omitted one of his classic remarks — which deserves to be preserved. To settle an argument as to the relative merits of two opinions, he said, "Why them two ain't no more alike than if you took a stone and trun it out in the middle of the road."

The defense rests.

CHAPTER IV

I NEARLY GOT INTO THE WRONG ARMY

*A*s preparation for nearly two years service in the French Army, I spent the previous six years studying German. It all started innocently enough. At Mamaroneck High School, the freshman class had its choice of German, French or Spanish. All three were taught by the same teacher — an attractive, young Irish-American girl who was always just one day ahead of her pupils and seemed to have no difficulty conducting classes in three languages in three successive hours — a fact that would have amazed the original Herr Berlitz.

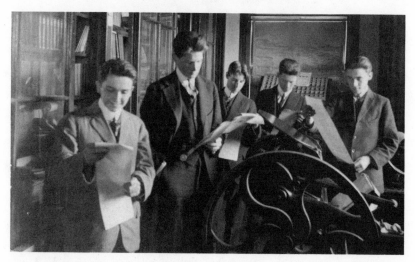

Printing "The Owl," our paper at Mamaroneck High, 1914.

Faced with this choice, I opted for German under the misapprehension that I already knew a lot of it. True, my maternal grandfather had emigrated from Sachsen-Meinigen in the 1850s and had found his bride-to-be in Bremerhaven while waiting for a boat that would carry him to the New World. My mother, her ten sisters and three brothers, spoke German at home. But their mother died when my mother, the baby of the family, was only six, and as the children grew older, the language became English. Most of the girls

Reba Greeman and Little Teddy with "Buster Brown" haircut.

worked, all went to high school — and only when "Papa" came to visit, a few German words came back into the conversation.

So my knowledge of German was less an asset than I had thought. In fact, it was a liability because my mother had no idea of German grammar. One of our first problems was the gender of German words beginning with the definite article. A sentence had been designed to illustrate this. "The girl (*das*

Mädchen) threw the fish (*die Fisch*) into the pail (*der Eimer*) of water." I may still have it wrong — but the idea is that "girl" is neuter, "fish" is feminine and "pail" is masculine. I tested it on my mother — she hesitated and then announced that the whole thing was ridiculous. "People who speak German don't go around saying 'The girl threw the fish into the pail of water.'" This was her final judgment.

Result, I got the poorest marks in German of all the subjects I studied in high school or college. I did get to speak it, however, and in 1916 when we had a boarder in our house named Otto Von Geissert, I spoke a lot of it. More accurately, I sang a lot of it. Otto and I, plus a schoolmate of mine named Charley Williams (he had one German-American uncle, a dentist, appropriately named Pickhardt) formed both a marching club and a *sangerbund* (singing society). So the quiet of Mamaroneck's summer evenings were broken by three hikers singing "*Ich hatte einen Kammeraden*" at the top of our lungs.

But then came the *Lusitania* (a British passenger liner torpedoed with the loss of over a thousand lives — most of them civilians, including many Americans) and a few related incidents — and only a little over a year later, I was negotiating with the French populace, male and female, equipped with a French vocabulary that began and ended with *éclair, bisquit tortoni, mayonnaise* — and other restaurant specialties traditionally offered in better-class places under their French names.

I bought my first French-English dictionary a month later when we had actually arrived in France and gone on duty with a French divison. But our first evening, my companion and I pointed to our mouths when it got to meal time and were escorted to the mess line. The first important words I learned were "*à la soupe.*" The second were of course "*Voulez-vous couchez avec moi, ce soir?"* even though they were not much use in a *poste-de-secours* (a first aid station).

I really worked hard on that little book, and I talked a lot of French although I had a tendency to slip in a few German words. It seems that the foreign language department of the brain has room for only one language at a time. Thus when I first spoke to German prisoners some months later, I alternated between *"Wo von sind vous?"* and *"D'où êtes Sie?"*

Which brings me at some length to two German stories.

In the spring of 1918 — when the war heated up — we really moved those ambulances and frequently had German wounded to haul. French wounded had priority, but otherwise everyone got the same lousy, bumpy ride to the base. On one of these multi-national trips, I had M. Levi, our interpreter, with me. He was a real linguist except that he mispronounced most English words, having learned them from books. We picked up a young German, not severely wounded, and Levi pointed to me and said, "What do you think of your chances of winning now that the Americans are landing?" "Nonsense," the German replied. "These are Englishmen or Canadians — there are no Americans here — the U-Boats have sunk them all." But Levi brought me over closer and pointed to my buttons, marked "U.S.," and then motioned to a half dozen more who were standing near, similarly uniformed. The youngster paused and sighed, and then answered *"Wissen Sie, da von hat Mann uns nichts gesagt."* (*"You must understand, nobody ever told us about that."*)

A prime example of the German mind — before, then and since — if you are not told it's so, it doesn't exist. They told them twice "The Yanks are <u>not</u> coming," but come we did. And the Fatherland lost two world wars.

A short time later, I had two wounded Jerries in the wagon and was waiting for a third to make a full load. Our Ford ambulances carried two stretcher cases on the floor alongside each other and one hanging on straps above and in the center, so he could bleed on both, impartially.

I had a kid with me named Parnell from West Virginia. He was a recent replacement — he had only been in France a short time. He spoke no French or German — in fact, his English was not too good. He noticed a ring on one of the prisoners and asked me to get it for him — offering a pack of Camels in exchange. I did not hesitate because I knew that when the Germans got to the base, they would be stripped of all their valuables by the vultures there who ran a souvenir shop on the side. Also, the ring was a horseshoe nail with an Iron Cross stamped on the head — worth about a quarter.

But the young Kraut started to put up an argument that his mother had given it to him, and it was his good luck charm. I was about to desist when his companion, a *Feld-webel* (Sergeant), turned his head and said one word, "*Gibts!*" ("Give!"), and the Private quietly took off the ring and turned it over. Of course, we gave him <u>two</u> packs of Camels.

But it was a lesson in German Militarism. We discussed it later, and all agreed that two American wounded prisoners would not pull rank — nor two Frenchmen either. That was how it was in 1918 — we didn't know then about Algeria or Vietnam. I wish we had never learned.

P.S.

Besides studying German and then working for the French Army, I became particularly fluent in German right at the wrong time.

With the Declaration of War, in April of 1917, anti-German feeling began to rise — "German fried" potatoes became "home fries" (and remain so to this day). Laws were enacted to restrict the movements of enemy aliens. I know because we had one living with us.

Otto Von Geissert, two years my senior, was a perfect specimen of the Teutonic tribe — sentimental, hard-working, obedient, strict — you name it — he was the embodiment of his heredity and environment. He was also my father's assistant and a good typist, and Dad wasn't about to lose him. After all, we lived a full mile from Long Island Sound, and it wasn't likely that Otto would sneak down to the Larchmont Yacht Club to signal his pals coming into the harbor on a U-Boat. Besides, the Yacht Club didn't admit Jews, and Otto wasn't really "Von" Geissert — we only called him that because we loved him.

April moved on and May, 1917, arrived. I was still at N.Y.U., although I was already in the U.S. Army and had an identity disk. My number was #9292, so I must have been among the first ten thousand to join up after Mr. Wilson made his speech regretfully announcing that a state of war existed. Every day, we expected a call to arms — or stretchers — but the top brass was not concentrating on ambulance drivers that month. (For one thing, someone named Lenin was making noises in Russia.)

Back in Larchmont, I had one problem that overshadowed all others — I was about to go to war and leave my baby sister more or less on her own. She was then, as she was all her life, very capable of coping with the world, but I was haunted by a large patch of poison ivy that grew in our back yard and which, I was sure, she would fall into.

Being a Boy Scout, I knew what to do and set about to do it. I put on long pants, a sweater, leather gauntlets and a stocking cap, and with shovel and ax I dug up and chopped up that poisonous growth. All would have been well, but a fly lit on my cheek (I was perspiring heavily), and I dislodged the fly with my gauntleted hand — well soaked in the poison of the noxious weed. I became infected. I was soon, in fact, one great blister. My face and neck were wrapped like the mummies of old, and that night came the call to arms!

About 5 o'clock the phone rang, and a fraternity brother told me that he had seen some of my fellow volunteers on their way to the nearest armory. It turned out they had found a crap game, but, nevertheless, he felt that I should come and find out, lest I be A.W.O.L. even before I was mustered in.

Of course, I couldn't drive — hell, I couldn't see. But there was always Otto and my father's Studebaker — a seven-passenger, four-cylinder touring car that looked like something used by an international spy ring. So we took off like a bat out of hell for N.Y.U. "uptown" — the city college in the country — down the Boston Post Road (little changed , back then, since it had been the Kings Highway in George III's time) through Fordham.

Of course, we were speeding — 25 or so miles per hour. (I think, in retrospect, the limit was 20 and 15 in Van Cortland Park.) And, of course, we were stopped, and the officer, true to his tradition, must say, "Where do you guys think you're going, to a fire?" To which Otto, not recognizing the rhetorical question, replied, in his thick accent — "No, Sir! But ve are on our vay to de army to fight for our country!" and the cop broke up. "Just which army and which country?" he wanted to know. Of course, we became friends after that, and I emerged from my cocoon of bandages to prove that we were all on the same team. But it was close.

To return to our resident enemy alien, my pal Otto, you should know that in the spring of 1917, when most patriots were busy cor-

43

recting restaurant bills of fare, renaming *"sauerkraut"* as "liberty cabbage," there were still enough hardy souls to enact legislation to protect us from enemy submarines. (Actually, in 1916, a German sub *had* surfaced in New London, Connecticut, to purchase certain needed medicines for German children. Her reception was mixed. Some saw a threat to our neutrality. Others praised German ingenuity for running the British blockade unscathed.)

But one article in the new orders was a beauty. It forbade enemy aliens from traveling within a quarter mile of the sea coast. Thus, a German living in Manhattan could not take a ferry to Jersey or Long Island or, if on foot, go west of Tenth Avenue or east of First. In retrospect, it may have been 100 yards, not a quarter mile, but the intent was obvious — to prevent spies from signaling to U-Boats.

At that time, my father was employed by Morimura Bros. — a leading importer of Japanese wares. This was World War I. We all "knew" that our allies, the Japanese, were little yellow monkeys that copied everything — including American "know-how" — but we didn't know they could locate Pearl Harbor until much later. By the same logic, my father's assistant — Otto Von Geissert was obviously a goose-stepping son of Kaiser Wilhelm — albeit an excellent typist and stenographer and full of admiration for everything American.)He later became a citizen and a prosperous baker in Seattle, Washington, a good husband and father.)

Fortunately for all concerned, Morimura Bros. was on 23rd Street between 5th and 6th Avenues — almost the geographic center of Manhattan Island — midway between what was mistakenly called the "North" River and what was correctly called the "East" River. Thus, Otto could do his chores and sleep in our house — well away from the treacherous shores full of blinking lights and oddly-shaped docks suitable for subs.

One such facility was discovered on Milton Point, near Rye, New York. Apparently, some lover of boating enjoyed a fast motorboat which he berthed at water level in a structure designed to go in and out of with little or nothing showing. My father had joined the Home Guard to do his bit after not quite graduating from the Civilian Infantry School at Plattsburg, New York. One night, he and his neighbors descended on this innocent Westchester boatman crying "Submarine Base!"

P.S. — He had a German-sounding name, but it never made the Times — not ever the *Mamaroneck Paragraph* — our local *Tageblatt.*

Teddy and Theo. Too young to fight.

Question? Did anyone ever try to prevent enemy aliens from living in Hoboken? After all these years, the question is moot.

CHAPTER V

VITAL STATISTICS I —
THE AVERAGE LIFE SPAN OF A MAN AT
THE FRONT

*N*ow a little essay on Vital Statistics. In the period between 1914 and 1917, there were no radios or TV sets, so adult education was achieved primarily through the Sunday magazine sections of the great metropolitan dailies — such as Hearst's *Journal-American.* Here, you would find illustrated articles on "Going to the Moon," "Boring a Hole through the Earth to China," etc., etc. One of the favorite topics, after August 1914, was ghoulish — "The Average Life Span of a Man at the Front." This could be broken down into "infantry," "cavalry," "artillery," etc. Eventually, they came down to "ambulance drivers" and came up with a figure — of seventeen days!

In August of 1917, some 550 of us, destined for that purpose, were aboard the *S.S. San Jacinto* enroute to France. And this was one of the prime topics of conversation. We had an extraordinary trip across on several counts. For one thing, the sea was like a lake — no storms, no seasickness. The boat, a United Fruit Company "banana boat," had cabins for about 24 people. These became the officers' quarters. Below decks, some ingenious architect had transformed the cargo holds into quarters for the enlisted personnel. (The draft had not yet gone into effect — which is another story — because a year later some newly-arrived draftees accused us of having enlisted to avoid the draft!)

Those accommodations deserve the pen of Dante and the

brush of Gustave Doré. By running parallel lines of pipe with canvas stretched between for hammocks, in three tiers from floor to ceiling, they had improved on the sardine can. The ventilation was the hatchway that extended right down to the keel and housed the ladders by which we climbed up to the deck and down to Gehenna.

Once on deck we had only one problem — regulations. To avoid being spotted as troop ships by enemy subs, we had a rule that you couldn't go within three feet of the rail. Maybe there was some other reason, but the fact is that we sat or lay along the superstructure, still like sardines, but without the oil — for thirteen days, between Hoboken and St. Nazaire.

That's why there was so much time to argue about our seventeen days and what to do with them.

I have mentioned that we were a motley crew — ranging from pampered millionaire's sons to Bowery bums. In between, somewhere, was Flitcroft Evans — an older-than-average bachelor, fond of telling how he sold Crisco to Jewish housewives who suspected that it was lard. Like most good salesmen, he was his own best customer. He was sold on the seventeen-day statistic. It was then the middle of August, and he figured just half the section would have Thanksgiving Dinner that year.

He also believed in reincarnation — so for him dying was like changing trains on a long journey. I hate to report that he lost his belief and his sang froid when the first shell exploded in his vicinity. He did his job though, albeit he was thereafter known as anyone could have predicted — as "Shitty Flitty."

Going back to the 17-day prediction, obviously, this figure was wrong, but it took us nearly two years to figure out why. It was Goethe who said a man was lucky if in his lifetime he had ten minutes of complete happiness. This is the same type of bad figuring and is based on the same wrong premise. When 34 out of 35 of us from SSU 592 came back to the U.S.A., we knew the answer. It goes like this — we were in the army for 23 months — but overseas for only twenty. Five of those twenty were after November 11, 1918, i.e. the Armistice. That leaves fifteen — and we were a month getting into the war zone after landing in France at St. Nazaire.

Parenthetically, we were attacked by subs the day we landed but suffered no casualties. If we had, it could not have been counted against the seventeen days as we were not driving ambulances. About that exciting adventure, please see the enclosed clipping from the *New York Times* which is transcribed for your convenience. (The publication date was December 12, 1918. The blank spaces indicated by lines are original censorship marks in the newspaper brought on either by the exigencies or war or a desire to maintain privacy.)

TALES OF U-BOATS SUNK IN BATTLES BY OUR FLEETS

Letter from an American Boy Which Reaches The Times Says Nine Were Destroyed

----

"BODIES OF 47 HUNS" IN SEA

Writer Says Five Transports, Six Destroyers, and Two Airplanes Attacked the Enemy.

49

ERROR IN NAVY BULLETIN

Department Reports "All" U-Boats Lost In Recent Fight When "One" Was the Fleet's Toll.

Two reports of attacks on American transports by German submarines became current here yesterday. One was a dispatch from Washington given out by Secretary Daniels, which first contained the information that six U-Boats had been sunk in the encounter, and later corrected by the Secretary to state that only one submarine had been destroyed; the other, a report in the form of a letter which reached THE TIMES from an American boy now serving at the front.

According to the corrected statement given out by Secretary Daniels from Washington, the American steamer Westwego reported to Paris that on Sept. 5 several American ships were attacked "while cruising" by a massed force of six submarines. One of the submarines was probably sent to the bottom.

The American boy's letter, dated Aug. 25, told of the sinking of four U-Boats on one day after an attack on transports, and the finding of the bodies of forty-seven drowned Teuton seamen. Then, the letter continued, the next day a fleet of destroyers sank five more submarines.

His letter follows:

> On Active Field Service With the
> American Expeditionary Forces.
>   Aug. 25, 1917.
> Dear Dad: This is deep stuff. This is the
> positively last letter you will get except cen-
> sored field postcards. One of the garbs (sailors)
> on a returning transport will get it to you.
>   The news I have is big. We came over on
> the _____, a _____ Line tub. But we had a very
> good passage, only two days' rain. On the last
> morning, when twenty miles from land, we
> were attacked by twelve submarines. There
> were five of us transports, six destroyers, and
> two airplanes. We got four subs — forty-seven
> dead huns floated in the next morning — and
> we didn't lose a ship or man. Yesterday the
> destroyers went out and surprised the subs at
> their base, getting five more while they were up
> for air. The prisoners are just coming in. Kids
> about 16-17 years old and old men. Some
> army.
>   But we have lost some freight steamers late-
> ly. Result our army Y. M. C. A. is short of
> candy, cigars, &c. We have been buying very
> good cheese, bread, and white wine, however,
> so don't worry about our insides.
>   We are in _____ now, in a camp of infantry,
> cavalry, artillery, &c. Our section goes first
> again, next Thursday to _____, and then _____
> miles from the front. Some class to us.

51

We do not get our salary for two months.
That's the overseas system. Pay every second
month. And, believe me, things are high. The
French storekeepers tell us frankly they have no
desire to cheat us, but are charging double so
they can live through the Winter. Believe me,
they need it. So you send along some dough,
and it will go for a good cause.

I am in excellent health as are all the boys.
We might be in Plattsburg if it were not for the
different language. Conditions are almost identical. Seacoast, bathing, (this was once a swell
watering place — French cafés open on the
boulevard — all that sort of thing.)

I shan't write any more now. You know
everything there is to know. I'm taking no
chances. I have just enough sense to keep clean
all around so you need not worry on that score.
Or for that matter you need not worry on any
score. This is a safe place, believe me.

I am not writing to mother, _____, _____ or
any of the boys. This will have to be a sort of
circular letter because I can only get one
through. But you pass the news, dad.

Give my dearest mother all the love in the
world. I can't express my feelings, as you
know. All my emotions get clogged up and
choke when I try to write them. But I know ma
is being brave and not worrying. And as for my
fat kid vampire sister, dad, well, if she doesn't
stay healthy and send me lots of candy I'm
going tell Ol Jemimah. Give my love to

_____.. Tell her she will hear from me soon.
Write to _____ or somebody in the frat. Their
addresses are all in the _____. Tell them all to
send cigarettes. If I don't use them, some of the
poor fellows will.

That's about all, pa, except for love and
kisses and all those pretty things for my relations, friends, enemies, &c. Your loving son,

Teddy.

BACK TO STATISTICS

Anyway, we still had fourteen months of active duty —
except for the fact that all troops are rotated between active duty
and what the French call "repos" and we were on repos for at least
half the time — which leaves seven months.

Now when you are on duty you may be one of the four cars
that go to the first aid stations, or you may be one of the sixteen
cars at the base or on reserve. This cuts down 80% of those
seven months, leaving about forty days all told — that is when
you are under fire, if there is any firing going on. After all, there
was the fall of 1917 and 1918 right up to March, when both
sides were waiting for something to change. Even the British had
given up sending thousands of men to certain death to capture
200 yards of mud. The Germans gave up that kind of warfare
after Verdun. And the French couldn't have mounted another
offensive after General Nivelle, "The Butcher," had done his
stuff. So I guess we are down to about twenty days that are dangerous, and, if you last through seventeen of them, you are in the
clear. It must be so because the man we lost, Joe Broadfoot, had

to transfer to the tanks to get himself killed.

We did have a few wounded and a lot of gas but no deaths at the Front. Section 594 lost two men — and the whole corps about 100 out of 3000 — so the odds-makers were not that wrong. They just made it sound worse than it really was.

P.S

MORE ON SHITTY FLITTY

Another comment about Flitty. In retrospect, he was an avowed pacifist — an early member of the "conscientious objectors" of subsequent conflicts. At a later date, Flitty would have been more articulate in his opposition to war. Then, we just thought he was a "sissy."

This brings us to another thought. He was probably a homosexual. His comrades never discussed it. At that time, unless a man used rouge and dressed up like a girl, we knew nothing of what went on in the minds of a substantial percentage of the male population. This has changed dramatically in a few years — to the point where we have large organizations of "Gays and Lesbians." This, too, has put a difficult requirement of honesty on quiet conformists like my poor comrade, Flitcroft. What could his mother have been thinking of when she gave him that name?.

CHAPTER VI

VITAL STATISTICS II —
LIFE AND SEX IN THE A.E.F.

*T*his is a short history of the love life of the A.E.F. or, more particularly, of SSU 592. With a membership of 35 First- or Second-Class Privates, we attained a respectable level of lubricity — thirteen cases of VD or a little better than one out of three. You may remember when "four out of five get pyor-rhea." We had that too — it was called "trench mouth" — and "Sister Di" of the three "rrhea" girls was always present.

I went bathing in the Marne after the Second Battle that bears its name. My ablutions were cut short by a corpse floating down its not so limpid waters. Result — diarrhea that almost reached dysentery. I was saved by my buddy Charley Williams who obtained (I do not say purchased) a whole hand of bananas which he fed me until I was physically plugged up. But this little story is about the third sister — gonorrhea — and our joint approach to the problem.

The powers that organized the Army overseas knew which side was up — they used G.O. (General Order) 45 which stated briefly that any soldier who contracted a venereal disease and had not visited a prophylactic station after exposure — and received treatment — was subject to court martial and could, if found guilty, be sentenced to the brig for 90 days and fined two-thirds of three months' pay. Note the consummate delicacy of this pro-vision — not two months' pay — that would leave him broke, but two-thirds of three months' pay — the same amount, but he would get some money every pay day. Maybe just enough to get to the nearest whorehouse. (By the way, in case you were wondering, our salary while overseas was the famous "33 dollars a day, once a month.")

There was always an argument whenever one of our boys started to leak a little whether he had gotten a "dose" or whether it was an old one coming back. Every rookie was told the Army's traditional attitude toward this mixed blessing of the goddess Venus. A — "It is like a bad cold, only your nose doesn't run," or B — "A man isn't full grown unless he's had the clap."

The American Army went further than old wives' sayings and general orders. They set up elaborate prophylactic stations in the cities where there were lots of troops and lots of girls. I saw one in Bordeaux as big as a men's room in a metropolitan railway station. They had stalls along a 50-foot wall with half-gallon tanks of potassium permanganate hanging on the wall and rubber hoses to insert in the appropriate orifice. The fact that these were communal didn't bother anyone as it was assumed that the solution, commonly known as "red pepper" was itself a germicide. The French slang for the ailment is *chaude pisse* (hot piss) — a most accurate description.

The "girls" in the French houses of prostitution — legal and regulated in that time and country — were not the worst source of diseases. For one thing, they were inspected by a team of doctors once a week, and they "examined" their clients and took precautions against being "laid off," so to speak, as any prudent worker would do. But the trouble was that a lot of the boys, trained in the rumble seats of those early cars, would not "pay for it" in the Continental fashion. They wanted romance and got it — along with a souvenir — from some farm girl or lonely woman in the little villages where we were stationed. Even when they went to the houses with the big numbers on the door, they didn't observe the protocol. (Some of the bordels had red lights

— but that was for night-time. By daylight the distinguishing feature was *Les Gros Numéros*.) When we had been quite a while in France, and my command of the language was fairly good, I was importuned by the girls in one house where we often passed the time to explain to my comrades that they did not need to tear the girls' clothes off in their heat — they would gladly disrobe — or stand on their heads for that matter. But the boys wanted to feel that they were "making out," which involved some show of coyness by girls who were handling twenty or more clients a day and had to pay for their own finery.

In the larger cities, especially where the B.E.F. (British Expeditionary Force) was stationed, there was always one house in the line that was posted "for officers only," but in smaller towns that had just one *maison de joie* there was a problem. They solved it with true British phlegm. The house, with perhaps six or seven girls, was reserved for commissioned officers from 2 to 5 p.m. every afternoon — and all evening for enlisted personnel or "ranks." This produced a Dante-esque situation because the men outnumbered the officers fifty to one. So the lines of men converging on the door at 7 or 8 p.m. were like the run on the box office of a hit show.

One particular house — it may have been in Doullens — is etched in my memory. It had an outside staircase to the second floor — in French, the "first floor" — and on it could be seen in the twilight and until "lights out" at 11 p.m. a double line of men — English, Scotch, Irish, Australian, Canadian, French and American — chatting and lying to each other while they moved up a step at a time. The girls in that house never got dressed — even in the wrapper or peignoir that was their uniform. But I must add that in most instances they put on an act — unbelievable as it sounds — so that every customer felt he was being waited on. Unlike their American counterparts, they were never coarse and indifferent. But in the tradition of "Camille" or "Nana" they made love. *"Faire l'amour"* is the euphemism for what they did.

In our own little outfit, 35 men and a First Lieutenant, these matters were not so carefully regulated. In retrospect, I guess the Lieutenant wanted his outfit to have a good record. So there was no talk of court martial and no report sent to Paris headquarters unless a man had to be hospitalized. We signed our own "propho" slips — or that of a friend — and all was kept quiet.

One man broke the silence. Lawrence Whitney Collins, our patrician, from what was then the fashionable section of Brooklyn, was all that F. Scott Fitzgerald was to portray much later on. He was handsome and witty and played the piano by ear. He and a couple of pals "liberated" a baby upright which was stashed in an ambulance and transported many kilometers while we were out of the lines, and Larry enlivened our evenings with everything that Irving Berlin was writing. In the British sector, he had a mishap. He had imbibed freely and decided to go to town, but turned his car over on the way and was returned in disgrace — with his leg in a cast — not broken but badly bent. He took it philosophically. "I was on my way to the whorehouse," he said, "and would most likely have gotten a dose of clap, so this broken leg is a blessing." Good thinking — but to no avail. An old (?) dose showed up while he was confined to the back of his car, convalescing on a nice clean stretcher.

The Lieutenant of that time was a fragile young man named Willie Smith, who never should have had so much authority or so many problems. He was our senior, and only, officer, and it bothered him that many of his command were older and more worldly. After inspection in the morning, he would make the rounds of those temporarily incapacitated — and when he got to the back of Larry's rig, he would lift the canvas flap and say,

58

"Private Collins — how is your 'thing' this morning?" And Larry would take it out and shake it at him — much to his embarrassment — and describe his symptoms in lurid detail. He even wrote a song — to the tune of "Oh Beatrice Fairfax what shall I do?" which ran "Oh Private Collins how is your thing?" etc.

But the purple fluid must have worked. I knew all of the thirteen and saw them return to America and marry and die, and none seemed to be the worse for their amorous dalliance. In fact most of them boasted about it.

P.S.

I was lucky — and stayed away from foreign entanglements. I did have a girl in Nancy who claimed she could not sleep alone. It seems that one night during an air raid on an airfield five or six miles away, some plaster from the ceiling had fallen on her bed. She concluded she should be covered as much as possible — preferably by a gentleman.

We never talked about money — she was a working girl, a waitress in a gin mill. But I did ask her what she would like for a present and she said "*Nougat.*" I like that kind of candy, too, and we ate about a pound of it between us. Then I asked what else and she said a nightgown — which seemed appropriate, and I went to the local Saks Fifth Avenue, most likely a *Prix Unique* or early Woolworth Store and purchased same. A couple of nights later, I asked her again. And this time she said "*Les Brillants.*"

This translates into "diamonds" — enough said — we were transferred out of town the next day. And I have not gone back.

CHAPTER VII

A TALE OF TWO OFFICERS I —
"THE NUMBER ONE MAN GOES TO THE
HEAD OF THE STRETCHER"

*A*t Camp Crane, formerly the Allentown, Pennsylvania, Fair Grounds, where we trained to become ambulance drivers, we were a living embodiment of William Jennings Bryan's argument against increasing our standing army. He said if war came, a million men would spring to arms overnight, and they did, but they had nothing but their bare hands to fight with. We were non-combatants, so we didn't need guns, but we did need ambulances and we had exactly two — for fifteen hundred men. Even the two we had bore no relationship to the field ambulances we eventually drove.

More to the point, we had only about a dozen stretchers, and this gave the Army a lot of headaches. In Army thinking, the most important factor in training has always been Close Order Drill — the familiar count off, "one, two, three, four." But, in the Medical Corps, the count is, "one, two, one, two." Then, the "ones" step forward two paces and pick up the head of the stretcher, and the "twos" pick up the foot and forward march — only they march out of step so that the incumbent will not be thrown off the stretcher. We spent most of the summer practicing this technique — only to find that the authorities differed and, subsequently, decreed that the Number One Man went to the foot of the stretcher!

This decision threw our commanding officer into a tizzy. The result of good French brandy, added to his normal fuzzy thinking, made him a potential "Captain Queeg," although he was never mean and bad. He suffered too much being alone with nobody to talk to, and by the time we went to work in France evacuating wounded men, all this nonsense was abandoned, and all we had was the memory of Lieutenant Mauser saying "Now the Number One Man goes to the head of the stretcher, or is it the Number Two Man?"

At Allentown, and subsequently in St. Nazaire, we had Advanced First Aid — that is, bandages and splints, the application thereof. But, again, when we got going, all that was thrown out. In fact, it was a court-martial offense to touch a wounded man — it being obvious that the man who changes tires cannot also change bandages. Along with this acceptance of the facts of life, our original officers, all M.D.s, were replaced by men trained in transportation.

As this became known, our own M.D. decided he wanted to go up the ladder a step and become a Captain. So he started studying the manual which the War Department had given him — to prepare himself for whatever examination he might have to face. But studying alone is a wearisome task, so he enrolled the whole section as guinea pigs for his quiz program. He only did it once. After explaining to us that this was good training — as we might all be officers some day — presumably if the Thirty Years War broke out again, he proceeded to ask the first question.

"If you were in command of an ambulance train called into a strange place to camp overnight, what would be your first job?" Of course, some wise guy answered, "Find yourself a good place to sleep," and Lieutenant Mauser indignantly rejected this as being a slur on the honor of an officer and a gentleman. The second answer was, "Find a place for the men to sleep," and this really got a better reception. "You are on the right track," he said, "but that's still not the right answer." We gave up at that point, and he proceeded, reading aloud, to give us the winning and only correct answer, to wit, "Find a place to picket the horses." It seems he was studying the manual issued for Teddy Roosevelt's Rough Riders, which had not been revised to allow for Henry Ford and his ingenious Yankee devices.

Lieutenant Mauser had another peculiarity. At sick call he sympathized with all and sundry. But, perhaps to discourage malingerers, he always had the same thing that you had. So, if the first man had diarrhea, he had it too, and if the second was constipated, so was he. Which would have made him the subject of some great medical research if it could have been followed through. Actually he had been a mine doctor — concerned primarily with broken bones and weekend drunks. His prescription for practically anything was aspirin — which didn't do anyone any harm.

I fooled him once by coming up with a French specialty called "*La Gale.*" This is a skin disease caused by a tiny spider that lives in straw (with which we stuffed our canvas mattress rolls). It tunnels under the skin like a mole under a lawn and itches like the devil. Aspirin doesn't help it — so I was hospitalized.

The cure is not a great problem. The sufferer is placed in a really hot bath — for about twenty minutes — and then scrubbed with what feels like a wire brush to get at the insect. This treatment, repeated daily with a sulphur ointment, is guaranteed to kill or cure both patient and parasite in a week.

I spent the week and was obviously cured — in a large hospital located in a nearby army barrack or *Caserne*. This building, like many others scattered throughout France, is the peacetime home of the army and similar buildings can be found in any European country where the normal number of men in training was always a million or more. It was a three-story affair of solid masonry with no fancy work to relieve its austere monotony. It made a prison look attractive in comparison. Inside, it was simply a long hall with wards stretching the width of the building, each with about thirty beds in two rows and a wood-burning stove in the center.

The wards were naturally divided by nationalities — as far as possible. Most were "*Français*" (French), a few "*Allemand*" (German) — because the French treated their prisoners of war as badly as their own men — finally, there was a ward labeled "*Étrangers*" (Foreigners), and that's where they threw me. It was December and cold, and the ones who minded the cold the most were the boys from the colonies — the outposts of the Glorious French Empire — the *Annamites* and the *Malagazy*. That is why I knew a little about Vietnam long ago — because these little yellow comrades of mine were from Indochina — and the black ones were from Madagascar — Asians and Africans, about a dozen of each, and me.

The Annamites were barely five feet tall. Their buddies from the Dark Continent were mostly over six feet tall, but they all had one thing in common — they were cold. Most of them had never seen snow, all had chilblains, and some were losing one or more toes — a painful and malodorous process. They greeted me with enthusiasm — particularly when they realized I wasn't French — and promised to keep me warm. This they did by stuffing newspaper in the window frames — like someone planning suicide in a gas oven — and then cramming logs into the stove until it glowed red all day and all night. Of course, we had very little oxygen and plenty of carbon dioxide. But someone came through the double doors every hour or so, and nobody died of it — although I personally slept about twenty hours out of twenty-four — without sleeping pills.

Communications were at a minimum — they none of them spoke English and very little French. But their feelings on basic things were easily understood. The war was denounced as an obvious punishment which the gods had sent down on a mad world — and they were right about that. They knew they shouldn't be where they were and by gestures and expression showed the differences between home and this abomination of a country. And, finally, they had no difficulty in showing graphically how the women of Madagascar were superior to the women of France, as a grapefruit is better, and bigger, than a lemon.

I did have visitors from the outfit — and they brought cigarettes. Everybody smoked them, turning the air or whatever was in the room to a lovely, gray-blue color. But there were no complaints, and it must have killed the spiders because I was discharged and proceeded to find a new place to sleep in only five days. But I remembered my pals of the *Salle des Étrangers* years later when colonialism was a dirty word. Unfortunately, my government didn't call our involvement by that name.

I am not suggesting that I was politically conscious at eighteen — my favorite author was Rudyard Kipling — but, like many others, I had the idea that the French handled such matters better than the English. They were known to be "color blind." But what I saw then soon dispelled that myth, although I was still a long way from the March Against the War in Vietnam, almost fifty years later.

One more episode involving our "first," Lieutenant, Roscoe Mauser, and we can exorcise his ghost from our memories. We had been in St. Nazaire about a week, and there was very little for us to do. After Monkey Drill (calisthenics) at six in the morning, we had "squads east and west" or the Medical Corps equivalent and were through for the day. Mauser needed his shoes soled and heeled and picked me to take them to town for that purpose. With his permission, I took a companion — it was a two-mile walk each way, but pleasant, and you might get a hitch. I chose blond, curly-haired Charley Williams from Mamaroneck, New York.

We had the Lieutenant's shoes cobbled and then bought a loaf of French bread whose aroma we could smell through the windows of the bakery. To wash it down we picked up a bottle of a popular French beverage — *cognac*. And, on our return to camp, having delivered the shoes, we repaired to a nearby hill where there was grass and trees — and the war seemed very far away. Then, emulating Omar Khayam, we proceeded to read passages from Mark Twain's immortal *Huckleberry Finn* while consuming our loaf of bread and jug of wine. Some time later — the sun having set in the west — we crawled back to camp. Neither of us could walk. We were completely "blotto" and slept for twelve hours. By chance, we had both been posted for sentry duty that night — and our Sergeant had altered the orders to provide substitutes.

But the Lieutenant knew about this, and, in the cold, gray light of morning, he called us to attention at his headquarters. He worked himself into a lather telling us he could have us court martialed for being drunk on guard duty — which we hadn't been — and ended his oration by saying "You two boys have put your head into the noose — one false move and I will pull it tight!" At this point Charley made a gurgling sound in his throat, and I burst out laughing, and we were dismissed — but the warning was not forgotten.

Three months later, Charley got his load on and enlivened our barracks with a little music — singing off key at the top of his lungs. It was after taps and lights out, and Lieutenant Mauser appeared in full panoply — slightly inebriated himself. He reminded Charley of the previous episode in St. Nazaire and threatened to bring up the charges he had not brought three months earlier. This violated Charley's sense of military justice, and he made a classic reply — which I will never forget. "You intimidate me," he said, "and I'll intimidate you. You bring charges against me, and I will bring counter-charges against you — for not bringing charges against me when it was your duty to do so."

This involved reasoning so convoluted that our poor mine-doctor-turned-commander-of-a-section-of-wild-ambulance-drivers threw up his hands in despair — and left it to the Sergeant to bring order out of chaos. But we missed him later when we got a belly full of real army discipline.

CHAPTER VIII

A TALE OF TWO OFFICERS II — "PRIVATE GREEMAN, YOU DRIVE TOO 'DARN' FAST"

*A*nother officer story is the saga of Robert W. "Willie" Smith, our second First Lieutenant.

In St. Nazaire we were in a genuine army camp — wooden barracks in parallel lines around a parade ground. Our home away from home was next to the Amherst unit, and that's how we met "Willy" Smith. He was their Top Sergeant, and when the bugle blew for assembly at 6:00 a.m., he popped up like a toy soldier and in about sixty seconds he faced a perfect line of obedient young men — all from that junior Ivy League college.

Meanwhile, on our side of the street, there was chaos. Our Top Sergeant, Lawrence J. McGinley, was a tall, bald gentlemen of about 25 or 6 who had graduated from high school at least eight years previously, and had made his own living in a multitude of legal but highly unethical schemes. Having amassed a very modest fortune, he had returned to the halls of academe and become the oldest freshman at N.Y.U. College of Arts and Pure Science.

His bald head stuck out above the rest of his class like a beacon. Inevitably, he became class president and if the war had not intervened might have become president of the college. But he settled for Top Sergeant of our outfit — which now consisted of a nucleus of college men with an agglomeration of taxi drivers, drifters, sol-

69

diers of fortune who were not so fortunate, and who all had one thing in common — they did not like to get up in the morning.

So while Sergeant Smith was saying, "All present or accounted for," Sergeant McKinley was hurling unprintable oaths at a line of half-dressed, bleary-eyed bums slowly drifting out of the sack and facing a new dawn. The contrast was obvious, and, as luck would have it, someone overheard Smith remark to a friend, "I would like to have that gang of ruffians in my command some day — they need some real discipline."

Of course, "Lady Luck" heard him say it, and six months later, when both Sergeants had gone through officer's school, we got Smith as our Lieutenant, and McGinley became Lieutenant of the Harvard unit. Before we leave him, it is significant that once, when we were in adjacent areas, some of us met Lieutenant McGinley with a few of his men and learned that he insisted that they all call him "Mac" and refrain from saluting unless there were Majors or Colonels around.

We inherited Lieutenant Smith on a Friday evening in Nancy. We were off duty — detached from one division, not yet attached to another — our only job was an occasional call to help evacuate civilian wounded after an air raid. Nancy had about half its normal population of 100,000 souls. It was only twenty kilometers behind the lines but considered reasonably secure at that time. It was winter and no grand strategy was in store on either side of the Front.

Saturday morning is traditionally reserved for "inspection." The troops are drawn up in line, and the commanding officer looks them over. We were a sorry sight. Almost no one had a regulation uniform. We had bought a lot of tailor-mades from the American Field Service boys who had proceeded us or patronized local shops. We had souvenirs like German "*Gott Mit Uns*" belts which often fooled the MPs into thinking we were officers wearing "Sam Brownes." Many of us had high boots with laces and others had *Chausseur Alpine* berets instead of the disfiguring louse-cages of government-issue olive drab. Those who still wore the uniform had modified it by turning in the neck of the blouse — military term for coat — to form a "reefer" collar like on a civilian business suit. This eliminated the stiff, tight neck band and made a space for a maroon four-in-hand tie — maroon being the Medical Corps color.

Smith took one look at this motley array and stalked off without a word, leaving us at attention. A few minutes later, he issued his first order — a five-mile hike through town to give us some much-needed exercise. So we formed a column of fours — the first in many months — and started down Main Street, Nancy. The population was aghast — they hadn't seen a parade since the Krauts held Nancy for a week in 1914, and we felt like idiots. But we hiked like Boy Scouts — which we were not. After all, we had two men who had been decorated for bravery and others who had seen shells explode in their immediate vicinity and felt that Saturday morning was a time for resting in the sack.

Now way back in the rear was a lad named John Green — known, at his own request, as John Bum. He was a two-fisted drinker, a very strong, tough Irishman, a loyal friend and a crack-erjack mechanic who could keep an ambulance going with a monkey wrench and a piece of wire. He was also a raconteur, and he proceeded to enliven our march by telling an old vaude-ville story — known to all of us and always welcome. It was part of the routine of an Italian dialect comedian in the days when we didn't know that dialect stories were demeaning — Frank Sinatra's father was still in Sicily, and Frank wasn't born yet.

The way the joke is told, the comic says softly, "Evera night I comma home, and I looka up inna da window, and I-a see my lit-tle Rosie, and I-a say, 'Hello Rosie,' and Rosie she-a answer me back in her-a nice-a-sweet baby voice, 'HELLO, POP!'" Of course, these last two words are shouted by the entire company, and if it doesn't sound like a great joke now, it did seem funny then. But the result was devastating. The Lieutenant up at the head of the column hadn't heard the preamble. But he did hear the shout, although he couldn't distinguish the words. And he made a terrible error — he started to run. He didn't go far — just a couple of steps. But we saw that he was scared, and that was his downfall.

He ordered the Sergeant to take over and get us back to our base. It was the last hike we ever took. He holed up in his little cubicle, and his own private war began. He was fighting us in addition to the entire German Army — and he was all alone. Unlike the other branches of the service where there is a chain of command — Lieutenant-Captain-Major-Colonel, etc., in the Ambulance Corps there was only a staff in Paris, headed by a Colonel, and then some fifty Lieutenants, each in charge of a unit, with nobody to talk to except his own non-coms — who are really not officers.

It was this poor misfit that had the bad luck to command our outfit as we went into Belgium for our toughest assignment. As an instance of his lack of ability to handle men, everyone had to be addressed according to protocol. Thus, "Private Greeman reporting that Cook Ketcham requires Mechanic Greene to repair the goulash cannon," instead of just saying "The stove is busted."

He tried at times to hold up his end. I personally drove him on a tour of inspection of the first aid stations. We hit a stretch of road that was a bad one — there was even a sign that said "*EN PLEINE VU DE L'ENNEMI*" ("IN FULL VIEW OF THE ENEMY"). I did not do any sightseeing at this point, and when we emerged unscathed, he was holding on with both hands and could only say, "Private Greeman, you drive too 'darn' fast."

After eighteen days at the Front, our division, which had been badly mauled, was relieved. We started to the rear, and Smith started his petty nagging all over again — blouses to be buttoned up, tin hats to be worn at all times, etc., etc. We gave him as good as he dished out, and a few days later he threw in the sponge. He left us — without permission and without an officer in charge — and went to Paris and asked to be relieved of his command. He was hospitalized and transferred back to the States, suffering from battle fatigue or "shell shock" as we called it. And we got a new man who cleaned out half a dozen hell raisers and ran a reasonably tight ship until we all came home a year later.

There is an epilog to the story. About five years later, I was having my hair cut in the Parker House in Boston. I looked in the big mirror framed with bottles of hair tonic and there, in the next chair, was Smith. "Aren't you 'Willie' Smith?" I asked. "Robert W. Smith," he replied. "But I think some of my men called me Willie." He was so right.

It was during the first years of Prohibition, so I couldn't ask him to join me in a drink, but we did have a cup of coffee, and I said "Mr. Smith, you are now working for a big corporation," — he had told me that — "and you are an executive. Now in your company there are troublemakers and goodie-goodies, but the bulk of the employees will go along with either group if you appeal to them on a man-to-man basis. You had just that kind of set-up in SSU 592. But you never used your head."

"Oh," he said, "I thought of that many times. But of course this is business, and that was the Army — and such a course was impossible — it wasn't according to Regulations!" Let us leave him there.

CHAPTER IX

RELIGIOUS OBSERVANCES IN THE A.E.F. — "NANA OF NANTES"

*A*s I have stated before, my religious upbringing was almost non-existent. Neither of my parents was devout, to put it mildly. We lived in a Christian community — without a temple — until I was twelve. Also, I went to Ethical Culture School — which in its day was very progressive. They taught evolution in the second grade and would have taught relativity if they had known about it. Don't misunderstand — I knew I was Jewish — in fact, the pogroms in Russia made me incline toward the Triple Alliance (Germany, Austria-Hungary, Turkey) rather than the Triple Entente (England, France, Russia) in the beginnings of World War I.

All this was changed abruptly by a notice on the bulletin board in St. Nazaire shortly after our convoy had deposited us in that seaport. It said, and I quote, "All Ranks of Jewish Religious Faith may obtain passes to attend Services in Celebration of Rosh Hashanah (that's Jewish New Year) on Application to their Commanding Officer." Suddenly, we Jewish ambulance drivers became religious, even pious, Sons of Israel. We were four out of about 100 in our barracks, and we put our heads together fast. There was, of course, a synagogue in St. Nazaire, a two-mile walk from the camp although you could usually get a hitch on a truck of some kind. But who wanted two or three hours to go to a place that we could go to almost anytime?

Our commanding officer, we had already discovered, was not too bright. He was a doctor of sorts — remember, at that time all

75

our officers were M.D.s as we were "medical corpsmen" in Army parlance. It was only later, when the authorities realized we were truck drivers, that we got officers who had been trained in transportation.

But to get back to Jewish New Year celebrations, it turned out that all four of us were of a particular sect whose orthodoxy demanded that we get 48-hour passes to Nantes, the capital city of Brittany — about an hours' ride by train and famous for its hospitality since the First Crusade. With tears in our eyes, we explained to our Lieutenant the story of Jerusalem and the bonfires that were lighted to mark the coming of the New Year, on the eve thereof. They could be seen for twenty miles, the story goes, and soon the next city would light up and so on throughout Israel and Judea. But by the time the last bonfire was lighted, it was the next day — so there was always a question as to which day was Rosh Hashanah — and so, in this year of the Christian Era, 1917, we had to have *two* days off to be certain we were celebrating the right one. Without hesitation, the good doctor signed the passes and we were off.

After an uneventful train trip, we arrived in Nantes. We even bought tickets, not yet having learned the magic by which we later traveled first class all over France — you spoke no French to the conductor and no English to the MPs. We found the synagogue and at least one English-speaking French Jew who greeted us warmly and invited us all for a drink after the morning services. We palmed him off on the oldest and most serious member of the quartet — who actually knew several prayers in Hebrew — and the three of us went looking for amusement.

There was a square that was obviously the place to go — the local 42nd Street and Broadway of 1917. There were the four sidewalk cafés, one on each corner, the little round tables and painted metal chairs and, best of all, women. Obviously, they were professionals — we did not expect the mayor's daughter, although it was traditional that every streetwalker was the daughter of a Colonel who would die if he know what she was doing for a living.

I hooked up with Nana, which, she informed me, was her name. Whether she had read Zola is doubtful, but her mother may have. She suggested that I buy her a drink, which I did, and we started making arrangements — in mixed French, English and an occasional German word. Nana was not bigoted — she may even have known it was a Jewish holiday. Eventually, we made a deal. I took her to dinner — at a moderately-priced restaurant (no stars in Michelin). We went to a show — there was a local vaudeville house — and then repaired to her apartment from which I did not emerge until ten the following morning, at which time I had a rendezvous with my buddies.

Her apartment was right out of "Gigi" — who was as yet unborn — and she was just a girl who liked a good time and didn't mind making a living out of it. When she found my name was Edward or *Edouard*, she squealed delightedly, "*Mais vous êtes le troisième.*" ("But you are the third.") And when I asked if, indeed, I was the third man in her life, she explained that I was the third *Edouard*.

So after dinner and the theater and a night of "love" and breakfast we parted — having arranged a rendezvous for later that day which I had no intention of keeping. "*Post coitum animal triste est.*" I had in mind a day of sightseeing — we still had 24 hours of leave, and I knew from my voracious reading habit that there were places to go in Nantes. So when the four of us gathered at the square, I became the Guide — a function I have been exercising ever since on numerous trips to Europe, Mexico and even Little Old New York. I knew that there was a certain Anne of Brittany, 1477-1520, who, to quote the *Britannica*, "had a great political influence in her day." In fact, she ruled the roost from her castle in

Nantes — which we presently visited, complete with battlements, dungeons and the like. "Kilroy" had not yet been there.

Tiring after many flights of stairs, we repaired to the other attraction for tourists of Nantes — the famous botanical garden, which features several thousand varieties of plants, flowers, fruits and other loathsome objects. Having found a park bench, we sat and waited for the plants to parade by for our inspection while we cooled our heels. Well they didn't do it — but, lo and behold, Here Came Two Doughboys (the A.E.F. was just beginning to arrive), and one of them said "Hey — is one of you guys named Greeman?"

I acknowledged, and he continued, "You had better get your ass down town to the main square — there's a broad down there, and she has your dog tag, and she is stopping every American *soldat* and is threatening to go to the American Consul whose car is always parked in front of the Café de Paris. Why the hell didn't you pay her?"

I didn't need any further encouragement. I beat all records for the 1000 meters with a hangover and sightseer's feet and found a tearful Nana still stopping all comers with my identity disk in her hand. She gave it to me gladly and scolded me for not turning up for our appointment. After a pause, I blushed prettily and confessed that the dinner, the show and her honorarium had exhausted my resources.

"What do you take me for?" said she. "Last night was your treat — tonight it's on me. After all, '*Vive la France*' and '*Vive les Américains.*'" And so it was, and we went to a less expensive restaurant and a café where there was free entertainment and home to bed.

And in the morning, I caught the train easily and got back to camp ready to attack another year with Rosh Hashanah well taken care of.

P.S.

She gave me her picture and I had it for a time, but it got lost in the shuffle — "*Tant pis pour elle.*"

CHAPTER X

TALES FROM A TRANQUIL SECTOR I — CREEPY CARRIE

*E*ventually we got word to move up to the "Front." It was cold — it was also five o'clock in the morning of a gray October day, and we hadn't had a great deal of sleep. We stumbled off the "Paris-Lunéville" train, and I think we were all good and scared. There was nobody about except a couple of railroad functionaries, and we could hear a rumbling sound that was not thunder.

We were still a hell of a long way from the trenches — and these were the finest trenches between Switzerland and the sea. They had been "improved" by succeeding waves of infantry with much time on their hands and had many creature comforts — although the word "creature" included vermin — that is, rats and bugs — but we didn't know that.

We were reduced to 35 men and a Lieutenant — all of us presently designated as SSU 592. No one ever figured out "SSU." The first part is easy — "*Section Sanitaire*" — but why not "*A*" for "*Americaine*" or "*E.U.*" for "*États Unis*"? But there it was. The "*U*" — probably for "United States" — was variously translated as "Useless," "Unwanted," etc.

We had started in Allentown, Pennsylvania, 3000 strong and our contingent, the second convoy of the A.E.F. — the first was General Pershing's "Pet"s — was roughly one third of the total, was still a thousand men either on the transports or in the camp at St. Nazaire. From there just a third, about 350 men, drove 200 ambulances — which we had personally assembled — to a place called Sandricourt, west of Paris. There we left them to be redivided as needed and, finally, ten sections of 35 men each rolled into Paris at 9 a.m., made ten piles of their blanket rolls and duffel bags in the Gare de L'Est and were told to be back at 6 p.m. sharp to take the trains for their ultimate destination, as yet unannounced.

The Gare de L'Est — terminal of the Chemin de Fer de L'Est — serves the northeast corner of France including the champagne country — Rheims, with its martyred Cathedral, Lorraine, whose capital, Nancy, had once belonged to the King of Poland, and the Vosges mountain country right down to the Swiss border. That much we knew, and we were excited, nervous, scared and eager — all at once.

That first day "loose" with all of Paris before us, we were really very well behaved. We ate and drank sparingly and didn't go too far afield. In fact, at 6 p.m., 34 out of 35 were at the station. When we entrained at about 9 p.m., we were still 34, and the Lieutenant was having D.T.s and talking in terms of a firing squad for the missing man. But that man was one Virgil Miller, who was serving his ninth year in that man's army. He had been as high as a Sergeant twice and busted each time and was now a happy Buck Private. In fact, his sobriquet was "Buck" Miller. Nobody knew his name was "Virgil" 'til his white-haired mother came looking for him in Camp Lee, Virginia, nearly two years later.

Anyway, "Buck" showed up about midnight — claiming he knew when we were leaving better then we did — and showing the Lieutenant that his papers were in order, having been okayed by a Major a few hours before.

Later on, he explained this bit of Army Regulations which could be put to one's advantage if you are lost or strayed from your outfit — particularly in a foreign country. You approach an officer of the rank of Major or higher, any branch of the service will do, and you give him a beautiful salute — especially if you can stand up — and report that you are lost and trying to rejoin your outfit, and he will sign your papers to that effect and point you in the right direction and you are "home free."

So we were still 35 in Lunéville. Eventually, two trucks came to pick us up and drive us to Baccarat. These place names are familiar to more Americans today than they were to us in 1917. I eat off plates from Lunéville of a kind that have been made there for centuries — they are usually *pierre de fer*, that is, iron stone, and have an excellent reputation. The crystal of Baccarat is even more famous, and I can't afford it — though I have always admired it. Once, many years later, I visited their sales office in Paris and told them that I had slept in their shipping department for nearly three months. We used their loading platform for our ambulances — they were the perfect height. But no one offered me a cut-glass goblet as a momento — in fact, another war had intervened, and there was no one who could remember the ambulance service from the "little war" that we thought was so big.

Well the trucks drove into a courtyard surrounded by a high brick wall, and we were home. The *crystallerie* (glass works) was about 90% inactive. They still kept an oven going to supply surgical glass to the Army but, other than that, the men were at the Front, and the fires were banked. The administrative building was the local GHQ, and our ambulances were drawn up in a row under the inevitable double line of trees that set off the inner perimeter of the factory. This was almost a self-contained village — with rows of company houses varying in size according to the position of the employee — all centered around the big house, where the *patron* lived and all covered with ivy and the ingrained dirt from soft coal furnaces that had been there since the first Louis of France.

We were greeted by Unit 7 of the American Field Service — the Quaker-sponsored volunteer ambulance corps, whom we were replacing. They were veterans of at least two years' service and were the perfect models of a gentlemen's army. They bought their own uniforms — tailor-made by the best couturiers — they were the sons of Wall Street brokers and railroad magnates, among them if not Morgans, at least Goelets and Pells and Dana Vail of Postal Telegraph — a real cross section of Ivy League America. They had done a damn good job, protecting the "lifestyle" that they knew and loved and the system that had made them. Six months later, when the A.E.F. arrived in force, the war lost its glamor for the Rah-Rah Boys, and we who stepped in between the volunteers and the machine tried to salvage the best of both worlds.

They were going home as soon as we took over. Some who tried to enlist — now that the U.S.A. was a combatant — had to make the trip back through submarine-infested waters to do it because their draft boards had them marked A.W.O.L. But our main interest was in buying their equipment, and between actual cash and a few crap games we did pretty well.

For example, our beds were cotton bags of striped ticking which we carried rolled up and empty. The quartermaster or some Lance Corporal was supposed to find hay or straw, reasonably free of ticks and horse shit, with which to stuff them. But the Field Service had folding cots. We acquired them, and many other goodies, and none too soon as many of us got the *gale* — rhymes with "pal" — which is that spider that runs under the skin like a mole under a lawn and is not at all pleasant.

By nightfall all was regulated (*en règle*), and we gave them a farewell party (or they gave us a welcome brawl) at the Café du Pont, which was at the bridge that led into town. It was like a thousand others — it is always the Café du Pont — unless it is the Café de la Gare (at the railroad station) or the Café de L'Hotel De Ville (by the town hall). In good weather, there is the sidewalk café with its two or three rows of four tables — after all, you are not in Paris on Les Grands Boulevards. But inside it is warm, and there are benches and newspapers and upstairs in the private banquet halls ("We cater to weddings and funerals.") there is a piano.

We not only had plenty of talented musicians but, best of all, a man who could play anything if you could hum it, so from then on Lawrence Whitney Collins never had to buy another drink — as long as he could tickle the ivories and we could bellow.

The transformation from the cold, dark morning at Lunéville to the warm, well-lighted interior of the café was enough to turn all our heads. One detail in particular put the finishing touch to our first day in the war zone. The waitress, we soon learned, was known as "Creepy Carrie" because, with her long black skirt, she had a way of moving that has since been made famous by "The Partisans" — a feature of the Russian Moiseyev Dancers. No feet can be seen — just a sort of gliding motion, unhampered by two hands full of beer steins, of course.

She was pinched or patted from time to time. She was the local Madelon of whom it is written — "*Pour nous elle n'est pas sévère, quand on lui prend la taille ou le menton.*" Or "*Les Nichons*" — a French soldier's ditty about a legendary, compliant café girl who never scolded when we took her by the waist, the chin (or the titties). At any rate, she did boil over about midnight, and a brave knight from Mamaroneck, my hometown by the sea, offered to take on the American Field Service — one at a time — because they were affronting French womanhood.

Cooler heads prevailed and Creepie Carrie ended with the biggest tip of her career to date.

CHAPTER XI

TALES FROM A TRANQUIL SECTOR II —
THE MAN WHO WASN'T DEAD

I have mentioned that Baccarat, in Lorraine, where I spent my first three months at the "Front," was a very quiet sector of the line. But, from time to time, there were some casualties, and one such case had a typical O. Henry ending.

We were using Fiat ambulances, big ones, that had a two-man crew. So when we did bring in a wounded man, we hopped out and opened the back door (they looked like old-fashioned ice wagons that you could climb into), and then put the *blessé* on his stretcher on the ground in front of the hospital. At this point, a doctor would be summoned — they did not always come a 'running, especially at meal times — and he would make a perfunctory examination and then assign two hospital orderlies to carry the unfortunate victim to the proper ward or the morgue if that was his destination. This quick exam was the famous "triage" that you heard so much about on "M.A.S.H."

This particular man had a bad abdominal wound — he had been bandaged at the first aid post but was obviously in tough shape. The doctor listened with a stethoscope, held a mirror in front of his mouth, and then turned his thumbs down to indicate that we had a D.O.A.

The boys were ready to take the body off when someone in charge said "Where is his *fiche?*" Now a *fiche* is a piece of paper — unfamiliar to Americans of that era but all too familiar in these days of Social Security, Medicare, etc. It was in fact his identity card. So someone looked for his dog tag — which should have been hanging around his neck but wasn't. Then I put my hand in his trousers' pocket — whereupon he let out a noise between a shriek and a groan and literally jumped off the stretcher.

Obviously, he wasn't dead — although his heart had almost quit. Equally obviously, I had by chance touched an exposed nerve and galvanized him into action. He was taken to the operating room without further ado and miraculously saved. Those Frenchmen were tough. In fact he heard his own story from the orderlies and two weeks later got in touch with me, and we split a bottle of champagne at his bedside, much against the nurse's admonitions. "Whatthehell," said he, "better to die from champagne than a grenade," and I don't believe he did die — at least not of that particular battle.

One more note about the *fiche*. *Time Magazine* of September 2, 1974, reported that France has finally abolished the hotel version of the *fiche*. This was the paper that every guest filled out at the registration desk or very shortly thereafter. It contained your name, address, date of birth, parents' names and nationalities and, best of all, your *occupation*. This always amused tourists. When I traveled as a civilian years later, with my wife and her sister, I enjoyed myself by putting down a different occupation at every hotel — and we often played one night stands where my poor sister-in-law was variously an acrobat, a glass blower, a cowgirl or anything else that came to mind.

Just once, I asked a clerk what good this information was. I knew it went to the local police. "Aha," said he, "that is how we catch a crook if he lies about his occupation."

I have been thinking about his answer ever since. Did he mean that this *escroc* would put down "burglar" when he was in fact a pick-pocket? I leave it there. The *fiche* is no more.

CHAPTER XII

TALES FROM A TRANQUIL SECTOR III — "LET HIM GET HIS OWN PRISONERS"

*I*have mentioned that for the first six months of our private version of World War I we had it pretty good. Actually, if some super power had wanted to run a training program for new ambulance drivers, it couldn't have been better. The province of Lorraine, near the border of Alsace, is hilly if not actually mountainous. It had been taken by the Germans in the first onslaught of 1914 and then regained right after the First Battle of the Marne. When the French got to the hilly country they slowed up — and the loyal opposition took the hint and slowed down. It just takes too much effort to fight (old style) in that kind of country.

So for three years the trenches had stayed put while battles raged further north and west where open plains gave general staffs dreams of break-throughs, flanking movements, etc., and several million young men died. All this was to our advantage. We were settled in Baccarat where we had an actual hospital to serve our base. And our *postes de secours* were in houses — with stoves and electric lights and even occasional civilians who had sneaked back into the so-called "war zone" after evacuating in 1914.

This part should really be illustrated — with moving pictures in color — only they would be kind of slow motion. Take Badonvilliers, population prewar about 700 — a farming community — some vineyards, a church, a main street with about six stores and a cluster of barns, silos, stables and chicken coops. It was about 300 yards from the front lines. In fact there was one place on the main street where there was a gap between two buildings that was marked with a hand painted sign "*EN PLEINE VUE DE L'ENNEMI*" ("IN FULL VIEW OF THE ENEMY"). When passing on foot, you went fast. When driving, you went slowly so as not to kick up dust. Otherwise, you ignored it.

Every day, at about 6 p.m., a Fiat ambulance with a driver and an assistant was parked in the backyard of a two-story building in the center of town. And the car that had been there for 24 hours went back to Baccarat — about twelve miles — where the movie theater was open two nights a week and several thriving cafés, with pianos, seven nights a week. Of course, in the event of a casualty (once a *poilu* nearly cut his foot off while chopping wood) the car on duty would move.

Half way back, a reserve car would go up to replace it — and at the hospital a second car would move up to lie in reserve. But that was the exception to the rule — mostly you could count on 24 hours in Badonvilliers punctuated by excellent meals cooked by Madame La Farge (not her real name) whose house we lived in. Rumor had it that a Colonel was keeping her daughter, so he looked the other way when inspectors came around to see that there were no violations of the civilian regulations in the zone. But it never interfered with her cooking or our card game.

Just to keep up their franchise, the Germans organized an almost daily artillery duel during which shells fell and exploded in a nearby field — and the gallant French artillerymen answered in kind. We watched it occasionally from the church tower, which was our observation post — equipped with binoculars, maps, field telephones, etc. Once someone asked the observer why the Jerries didn't shoot at him. "Look there," he said. "That church tower three miles away is their observation post. We have a gun pointing at it in the courtyard below. If they knock ours down, we will knock theirs down — and then neither of us will have an observation post."

But all good things must come to an end. Sometime in December, 1917, our division got a new commander. His name was "Baston," and even though the English equivalent is closer than the French, he became known immediately as "General Bastard." He was not satisfied to let well enough alone. You see the XIV Division, to which we were attached, was a sort of French National Guard division. You might almost say "Home Guard." We had plenty of Gray Beards among us whose motto was "You won't end the war tonight — so lay low." Obviously, the boys on the other side were the same breed. But you were never sure when the German High Command would suddenly stick in the Crown Prince's own death-defying attack troops — so every so often you had to probe gently and try to come up with a couple of prisoners to read the numbers on their uniforms which identified their division.

This one afternoon we received the hitherto unheard-of request for three ambulances to report at midnight at our Badonvilliers *poste*. There was competition for the job. It sounded like an adventure, and, as I have tried to suggest, by that time we wanted action. The war was a bore — no blood, no medals, no fireworks — something was wrong. (Some months later we would have gladly gone back to Baccarat.)

But on this particular snowy night in the picturesque hills of Lorraine, we moved out and lined up like taxis waiting for the movie to end or the theater to let out. In the living room, two doctors waited with instruments handy — after all this was a first aid post — and so the minutes dragged. The *coup de main* was set for 3 a.m., and everybody knew it. In fact, it was firmly believed that the bartender at the Café du Pont in Baccarat knew every move that either army was contemplating and told everybody without fear or favor.

About 3 a.m., a shot broke the silence, and in a few seconds several hundred shots, as machine guns opened up on both sides. Simultaneously, star shells were fired and brilliant magnesium flares on parachutes floated slowly down illuminating the Christmas-card landscape.

Five minutes later the firing stopped. The lights went out — and two *poilus* stumbled into the room with cuts on their hands from barbed wire. They were our casualties.

"So what happened?" we asked. After a pause to be sure there were no high-ranking officers around, the reply came. "Somebody accidentally discharged his rifle when we were a few yards out — that gave the alarm — and the surprise raid was doomed. So we came back."

To put it plainly, General Bastard can go out and get his own prisoners. "*Vive la France*," and as we often added, "*Vive les Pommes de Terre Frites!*" ("Long live French-fried potatoes!")

CHAPTER XIII

R & R

OR

HOW TO MAKE THE MOST OUT OF A 24-HOUR PASS

*M*ost of our adventures during our visit to the Land of Lafayette and Louis XVI originated in the extraordinary way of life which had come down, almost unchanged, from the times of the above-mentioned. I refer to the bureaucracy, which included the Army, and which made it possible for those of us who were lucky enough to be linguists to accomplish a great deal with a minimum of effort or expenditure.

We had not been in action — that is actually attached to a French division — for a week before we learned what we needed to know in order to live under what the French call "System D." (We assumed because it is not as simple as A-B-C.) "System D" actually comes from the French "*se débrouiller*," meaning "to deal with a tricky situation, to handle things cleverly, to take advantage," and its less polite equivalent, "*se démerder*," meaning "to get yourself out of the shit." There is a discussion of "*se débrouiller*" in George Orwell's illuminating *Down and Out in Paris and London*.

For example, we had as commanding officers a French Lieutenant and an American Lieutenant. This French Lieutenant was in charge of the *Voitures Sanitaires* — that is the actual, physical ambulances — which, at that time, were Fiats owned by the French government. He could order that they be washed, but he couldn't order us to wash them. Only the American Lieutenant, who was in charge of us, the actual, physical ambulance drivers, could do that, and, of course, the reverse was true — the American Lieutenant could order us to wash, period, but not to wash property which did not belong to the United States Army — the ambulances.

We didn't need any more of a hint than that. The French Lieutenant was an amiable gentleman of a "certain age" — that is, too old for infantry duty. His job was considered a sinecure. Far from Headquarters with no Captains, Colonels or Generals around to plague him, he had a feudal fief, with his own valet, cook and clerk, and 35 Americans with their officer and his dog-robber and chauffeur, etc., his vassals. This was particularly appropriate because, we citizens of a democracy were surprised to learn, he was The Comte de St. Senoch — and was so addressed by his fellow countrymen in spite of the fact that France, too, was supposed to be a democracy.

He was replaced some months later by a gentleman of similar stature — The Marquis de Montalembert, descendant of a famous house, which included the world-renowned historian. Fifty years later, I stayed at the Hotel Montalembert in Paris — originally the *Hotel Particulier* of the family — that is, their town house.

But getting back to 1917, the knowledge that authority was divided was all we needed to avoid or evade unnecessary toil. We would alternately approach Lieutenant Mauser and say "That Frog Looie is yelling something at us, but I can't make out what he wants," and Mauser, fresh from setting broken legs and arms — remember, he had been a doctor in a coal mining town in Tennessee — would say, "Just salute him and forget it." Or we would give St. Senoch an elaborate salute and, in almost faultless French, advise him that our Lieutenant was being noncooperative as he had other duties for us to perform.

A variation on this ploy was used on every railroad to avoid paying for our tickets — and in even more interesting localities. For example, I once escorted four doughboys in the prime of health into the most luxurious brothel in Beauvais (right near the Cathedral) using the *livret matricule*, a kind of record book, in French, in which the tires on my ambulance were charged to me, with numbers, dates, etc., plus many official-looking seals. I just showed it to the American MPs at the door to the whorehouse (by that time the A.E.F. was there in force) and told them that I was in charge of these lads and was taking them to a special hospital and would sign for them in proper military fashion, by the numbers. (Lafayette had been in our Army, too, and left some of the old rules with Washington.)

But the best variations on the scheme were when the subject of furlough came up. After approximately six months of duty, an American soldier was entitled to ten days of R & R (Rest and Recreation), and he could spend it in any one of half a dozen places which the U.S. Army had chosen — and deloused and dried up for his comfort. They were all resorts — Nice, Aix-les-Bains, Vichy, etc., well away from the war zone and attractive enough — with lots of posh hotels — but alive with MPs and YMCA Secretaries and plenty of R & R — in this case "Rules and Regulations."

But a French soldier, after six months, got a one week *permission* or leave of absence to be spent at the home of his next-of-kin — wife, mother or even a cousin or uncle if he happened to be an unmarried orphan. Now seven days is less than ten days, but the French "Leave" did not include time spent going to and returning from the place of visit so it could be stretched to twelve or fourteen days without difficulty.

So we chose it. First, you picked a faraway place — in our case, three of us discovered an uncle in Pau in the Pyrenees — fifty miles from the Spanish Border. Second, while en route, if you saw a town that looked attractive, you got off the train and examined the local scenery, tasted the wine or other goodies and then lost your ability to speak French — and got on the wrong train and had to be helped and pointed in the right direction by a willing French officer who wanted to practice his English. The point being that as long as your papers were in order you were okay, and your papers were always in order if you had them stamped and signed and sealed once every 24 hours (after 24 hours you could be found A.W.O.L. — the other kind of "French Leave").

With this in mind, the trio to which I belonged planned it that way. We went from Nancy to Paris, to Tours, to Bordeaux, to Pau, all in a fairly straight line — but we took five days to do it. On the way back, we varied the route to include Troyes, which was a disappointment — it was nowhere near Albany, New York — but all told it was a hell of a trip, and we set a record for kilometers traveled that stood for quite a while — we could have stretched it, but we ran out of dough.

In between "leaves" — during periods when we were out of the lines, while our division was being brought up to strength, we had quite a number of side trips which we arranged on the flimsiest pretexts, always depending on how we could play the Lieutenants off against each other. They had an interpreter, but each thought he could dispense with his services. P.S. — they neither of them could.

One such "prowl" was a 24-hour trip that Adrian W. Ketcham and I took to Bar-Le-Duc — the source of the excellent *confiture* (preserves) of the same name that has graced the fine tables of two continents for a century or more. We never did find the jam factory, but we did meet a girl whose room, which we penetrated on some pretext, was decorated with pictures of herself on spirited horses, jumping over hurdles and winning blue ribbons. She was, in fact, an accomplished equestrienne, though this was not her only accomplishment. This episode, or one like it, is obviously the source of the well-known two-line story, "What's a nice girl like you doing in a place like this?" and the answer, "I guess I've just been lucky."

Another story that I have always liked, I first heard on that trip. Our train, a combination passenger and freight, stopped at a place called "Void." Of course, in French it rhymes with "Wad," but it looked like the English pronunciation — void of inhabitants. There was nothing visible but the station. Only on the horizon, about a mile away, was a church steeple and a cluster of buildings. Ketcham had been a paint salesman for Pittsburgh Plate Glass, and seeing this town, which the railroad had obviously by-passed, provoked this reminiscence.

KETCHAM'S STORY

There used to be a number of towns like this in my territory. You couldn't skip them because the customers would complain to your boss. So some fine June day with the thermometer about 90° you would swing off the morning train with two grips — a big one with your clothes and a smaller one with the order books and color charts and maybe samples of a new product. There were usually two trains a day — one in the morning and one in the afternoon — with about six hours in between. And if you missed that afternoon train, you had to stay overnight in some rundown flea bag of a hotel. Of course, there was no taxi.

So you would figure to leave the big bag in the station and carry the little one up to town. But the stationmaster had locked up his office and gone up to the head of the train to get the mail. But you would figure nobody was likely to steal your bag

97

between trains so you would just leave it there and start for the center of town.

You probably had three customers, and the first one had gone fishing — it being June — so you were relieved, and it only took ten minutes to leave him a little note that he was short of Green 1/2 gallons. The next guy was a doll. He said he had been expecting you and made out a little order so all you had to do was copy it in your book and give him a duplicate and say, "Thank you." That all took only another fifteen minutes and left you with plenty of time for the third man. So you would have a little lunch in the local greasy spoon and maybe smoke a cigar and then call on the last customer in town.

But that wasn't so easy. He wanted to buy all right but couldn't make up his mind. First he would want to know what was the trend nationwide — was barn red going to outsell chicken house green. And then there was a problem about gallons and half gallons — there was a price differential, but could the small customer pay it in order not to be left with a half a can of paint that would maybe dry out? All this was punctuated by customers who had to be polled on their opinion of what he should stock and so on and so on, with erasures and additions and the clock ticking. Finally, with fifteen minutes to go, you could close the book and shake hands and be off.

Halfway to the station you would hear the train whistling for the crossing, and you would start to run.

By the time you got to the station the train was there — but not your bag — because the stationmaster had seen it and locked it up in his office for safekeeping. But now he was up at the head of the train to get the evening mail. So you would run and fetch him and get your bag and start for the train which was now leaving — and with luck you would throw the bags up on the platform of the last car and jump — and maybe would take the skin off one shin.

Then you would get into the car and stow your bags and sit down and light a cigar and say, "By God and by Jesus I will never make that town again." And you would live up to your oath — for six months and then go through the whole performance over again — in two feet of snow!

That was Ketcham's story, and now the trains are gone, but there are still plenty of traveling salesmen, and that pain-in-the-ass customer is in every city in the U.S.A. In fact his name is Legion.

CHAPTER XIV

CHARLEY AND THE *AU PAIR*

*A*s told in a previous episode, a trio of *conducteurs des voitures sanitaires* (ambulance drivers) went on leave to Pau. On our first day of living in a hotel with hot and cold running water, we slept late and then made for the Boulevard Des Pyrenées. This noble avenue, lined with hotels on one side and affording a magnificent view of the Pyrenees mountains on the other, had long been a tourist attraction, especially for the British.

Sure enough, we heard English spoken and not by the U.S. Army. A charming Parisian girl of "a certain age" was tending to two British children, obviously of the upper class. We introduced ourselves forthwith, and, as we made an unwieldy crowd (three men and a girl), Ketcham and I allowed as we had to report to some nonexistent authorities and moved out. That left Charley and the *au pair* (our word is "governess").

When next we appeared, it was the following morning, and Charley did this tale unfold. They had put the children to bed, dined and promenaded, and, presently, hailed a cab and said "drive." Nothing loath, the chauffeur complied, and they had a petting session in the back seat worthy of Madame Bovary. After the ball was over, Charley said, "You had better put on your panties." At this point, she evinced complete surprise. She didn't know she had taken them off! When peace had been restored, he dropped her at her hotel and hit the hay, only to rejoin us in the a.m.

Naturally, we joined up for lunch and congratulated the loving couple, feigning to believe they were engaged. A few hours later, we explained that our leave was up, and we were A.W.O.L., subject to severe penalties — and lo, we were off to the trenches or a few miles behind them.

Six months passed, and we were off again, this time for Aix-les-Bains, a U.S. Army R & R dump full of YMCA huts. But we did stop in Paris where Claudette or Paulette lived — they were all named Paulette or Claudette. Charley had wired ahead telling her to meet him for dinner at the Hotel Bretagne — a name one of the older boys had given him as being cheap and clean.

Again we parted, and again Charley showed up in the morning — this time with a long face. It seems her father had seen the telly and knew the hotel as a brothel of sorts. She was allowed to go and come right home and ordered to bring her *fiancé* the following afternoon to her father's store.

Daddy had a *brosserie* — a store full of brushes, brooms and mops, in a residential section of Paris (Passy). He was a large man, and when we sidled in about noon he said, "*Entendez. Je suis rond, je suis franc, et je suis père de famille. Quelles sont vos intentions?*" (Translated freely, "I am a square shooter and father of a family. No double talk — what are your intentions?") During this tirade, Charley stood almost speechless. His French was vestigial. He managed only to say "*Quoi?*" ("What?") at intervals. That left it up to me. Never bashful, I stepped into the breach. "Calm your fears," I said. "My comrade wishes your daughter's hand in marriage." That broke the ice. Now the wine and cookies came out, and the picture of her brother, killed at Verdun. Soon we were all crying on each other's shoulders. This time we really had to get back to the outfit. So we made our *adieux* and went, forthwith.

Months passed. The Armistice was signed, and we were doing nothing in a farmyard in Fleury-La-Rivière, near Epernay. Charley had a new sweetheart, a woman of parts who made dresses for rich girls' dolls and liked her loving. But she had a social disease. Nothing daunted, they found new and fancy ways of making out, while I sat in the next room trying to seduce a girl whom we called "*la mitrailleuse*" ("the machine gun") because her words came out like bullets.

This little Eden was interrupted at 11 a.m. one fine day when a limo drove into our courtyard bearing an officer and a man in a frock coat and striped pants who identified himself as an attaché at our embassy in Paris. He was looking for a P.F.C. named Charles Williams who, his *fiancée* complained, was not getting her mail as she had not heard from him! Naturally, Charley said he had not heard from her, and the stand-off was broken when he sent her a flowery epistle, with his address in the States (wrong, of course).

This was not the last chapter. Two years elapsed, and I, not Charley, got the "Dear John" letter. She had always known how to contact us. She had made an unhappy marriage to a *poilu* (wounded) whom she pitied and was now running a *crèche* — a sort of daycare center for little children. Needless to say, we made a healthy contribution to the *crèche*'s upkeep — in the names of Cupid and Jeanne D'Arc, and so this romance ends.

CHAPTER XV

SOME OF US GOT THE CROSS OF WAR — *PARLEZ-VOUS*

*T*his is actually a story in two parts, entitled "How I Did Not Get The *Croix de Guerre*" and "How I Got The *Croix de Guerre.*"

Our first few months at the Front were spent in and around Baccarat, in Lorraine. As I have said, it was winter, and the country was hilly, and both sides were war-weary. There was a gentlemen's agreement in force — don't make waves — so except for a rare accident there was really no danger driving an ambulance in the middle of the world's worst madness up to that time.

Teddy celebrating New Years 1918 at Baccarat in top hat abandoned by evacuating French of 1914.

The spring changed all that — Russia got out of the war, and the United States got into it. I know we had been in since the previous April, but now we began to send trained troops into action. An often-repeated story — which might very well be apocryphal — had a Texas Lieutenant of Artillery firing his 75s within a few minutes of his arrival at the Front. A French officer is supposed to have run out in front of the gun waving his arms and crying, "Stop! Stop! It is not our time to fire!" True or false, it sounds typical of the way the war was fought on that "tranquil sector." Once a day a few shells exploded in a vacant lot on each side of the line — just to maintain the franchise.

The change came slowly. We had been in Nancy for several weeks, detached from our division. And now we got a new one — the French XVII, a division of the East — most of the men originally from Dijon and Besançon, that is, Burgundians. Of course, three years of replacements had destroyed the original solidarity, but they still talked as though they were better than Normans or Bretons or Meridionals (*Les types du Midi* — i.e., Southerners and allegedly lazy — an interesting comparison with the American South).

We also lost our lumbering Fiats and got Model T Fords — which we had assembled in St. Nazaire the previous September. They were a lot better suited to rough going as we learned later, but they were not as comfortable to sleep in — and no protection against flying objects. You could put your fist through the side of the body if you were really angry.

We started out on our new assignments at St. Clerment — only about twenty miles west of Baccarat, in similar country, but rolling hills rather than wooded ravines and little mountains — in short, better for fighting a war in. About the fourth or fifth day, we were on duty, we had three cars at a midway stop between the first aid posts and the base, when a call came in that an ambulance was needed in a little town about five miles away which we could actually see. We were on a hill, and it was in a valley, and large amounts of black smoke were visible in its vicinity. The French officer in charge said he would not order anyone to go in at that minute — his reasoning was that the firing would stop shortly, and the evacuation could then proceed with no danger to man or machine. But we were young and foolish, so we all volunteered to go at once, and Frank Kelly of Ossining, New York, and I won the toss.

We had no difficulty finding our way, and we were expected. We drove in, turned around in front of the *poste de secours* (marked with a red cross) and had the stretcher cases loaded as fast as I am writing this sentence. We also left without farewells and obviously were not hurt. Shells were still falling, but apparently the objective was a couple of blocks away — most likely the church which had a steeple and most probably was an observation post. So we hauled our tails out of there and went directly to the field hospital where we turned over our wounded — a Lieutenant and a Sergeant — and then reported to our barracks.

Our fame had gone before us. The other boys had reported watching us dodging shells on the road into the little town and back and our own French Lieutenant — the Count — now greeted us like prodigal sons returned from the dead, and in his best English pronounced, "You will get the Red Cross." (He meant "the Cross of War.")

We knew what he meant and were not displeased. Although we had actually done nothing but our duty, we were still Boy Scouts mentally and jealous of the boys with a chest full of medals. Believe me, we changed our minds later.

But we did not get the "Red Cross" although we were recommended for it. That same afternoon, a few miles away, a similar incident had occurred in another village which our division was defending — and at that place two of our boys, named Greaney and Hirschkorn, more or less duplicated our feat of prompt service and efficient rescue. But there was one difference — one of their wounded was a Major. So they had rank on us, and when the two recommendations came into Divisional Headquarters, theirs had precedence. As our English-speaking interpreter explained it — they didn't want to debase the value of the medal by awarding it too freely. So we were put in a file somewhere for later consideration, if we lived that long, and they got the medals.

Well we did live that long, and a lot longer too, and in another month we pulled out of Lorraine and after three days in box cars — the familiar *40 hommes ou 8 chevaux* (40 men or 8 horses, the carrying capacity of the box cars) — arrived near Amiens where the British Fifth Army was in real trouble. That trip was a saga in itself so I will skip it for the moment. We served a few days with the British, and then moved up into Belgium, and that is where we learned about the war.

First of all, the land was flat as a pancake, and the roads were straight as a string. This produced an obvious gridiron effect — so that when a north-south road crossed one going from east-west, you had perfectly square crossroads. And if you were trying to stop troop movements in that area, and had a halfway decent piece of artillery, you just shelled the crossroads and didn't waste ammunition on the space between. Also this territory had been fought over continuously for three years. We were about twenty kilometers from Ypres — the British called it "Wipers" — and looking down our throats was Mt. Kemmel — one of a string of hills which the enemy held and from which they could see what you were having for dinner.

Where we had been a few short weeks before, in Lorraine, the houses not damaged in the first battles of 1914 were still standing and in a fair state of repair. Our *postes de secours* were usually the

cellars of the largest houses in town — always stone and reasonably dry, warm and safe except for a direct hit — which was
unlikely when we were there. That too changed later. But in
Belgium, we had our first aid stations in dugouts with a mud
bottom, usually covered with water and everything else in pro-
portion. Instead of hoping that there would be no "business"
(that is, wounded to evacuate), you actually hoped you would get
a call which meant twenty kilometers back to the hospital and an
interval for coffee and some shut-eye before returning.

On this front, between May 12th and 30th (Decoration Day
— now called Memorial Day), we lost a lot of ambulances and a
number of men were gassed. This meant more work for the rest
of us — everybody except a few yard birds who made excuses for
not doing their job (Yes, Virginia, there are American slackers.)
did at least 24-hour duty and some even more. Every man in the
outfit deserved recognition, but, as previously mentioned, they
didn't want to give out medals like trading stamps. So four of us
were selected — at random as far as I know. And a month later,
when we were miles away, we were properly "pinned" and kissed
on both cheeks and presented with a large parchment scroll that
said, and I quote.

"Soldat Greeman, Edward, Section Sanitaire U. 592.

*" A fait preuve de plus grand sang-froid en évacuant des blessés du 14
au 28 Mai 1918, sur des routes violemment bombardées tant par
obus explosifs que par obus à gaz."*

("Demonstrated the greatest daring (literally 'cool-blood') evacuating wounded from May to 18, 1918, on roads violently bombarded both by explosive shells and gas shells.")

Decoration by Médecin Major. Next to me is Duncan Phyfe. In the front row are Lieutenant Harding, U.S.A., and the Marquis de Montalembert, Lieutenant in the French Army of the Republic.

(That's a Ribbon with a Silver Star.)

So I really was decorated for doing my duty — you could say that if I hadn't, I should have been liable to court martial. The other time when I volunteered and was cited for it I ran into politics. But it all averaged out. And I still had my medal some fifty years later when I marched down Fifth Avenue to protest the War in Vietnam, and I wore it and was interviewed by a reporter who wondered how a "hero" could object to giving his progeny a chance to win more medals. I told him — but it wasn't printable. At least it didn't make the headlines!

P.S.

I can't help but pass on a piece of news that came to me about Memorial Day — traditionally celebrated on May 30, until our omniscient government moved it to the fourth Monday in May — allegedly to give our workers a three-day holiday. In New York City, for the first time, this year (1992) there was no Memorial Day March. The paper reported that there were too few marchers last year — and they were all old and infirm. *Sic transit gloria mundi.* (Freely translated, "This place is closed on Sunday.")

CHAPTER XVI

AMERICANS EAT TURKEY FOR THANKSGIVING

*L*ong before we landed in sunny France, most of us had been pre-conditioned with respect to our Glorious Allies. Particularly, we all knew the stanza of "*Mademoiselle from Armentières*" that begins with the comment, "The French they are a peculiar race — *Parlez-vous.*" On the opposite side of the coin, we also knew that "Fifty Million Frenchmen Can't Be Wrong." Our thirteen days on the San Jacinto between Hoboken and St. Nazaire were enlivened by debates between proponents of both philosophies. Eventually everyone had to satisfy himself on these very personal matters.

But the peculiarities of the French had other aspects besides sex mores. They were, we soon discovered, both generous and stingy, open-handed and tight-fisted, as a few incidents will prove.

There was, in Baccarat, a kind of general store where you could buy pens and pencils and writing paper and handkerchiefs and toothpaste. It was an early version of the Five and Ten Cent Store, but the fixtures were the old glass-topped counters where each piece had to be taken out by request and then wrapped up or returned to its little corner. One of the boys, trying to get a better look at a pocketknife, leaned too hard on the glass of one such display and broke it. He was stone sober and all apologies and contrition at once — in fact he had his money out of his pocket to pay for the damage in seconds.

But the *patron* was an ugly peasant who resented foreigners of any persuasion and, as we frequently heard, "*Les Américains sont pires que les Boches.*" ("The Americans are worse than the Huns.") So he proceeded to denounce our boy as though he had raped his daughter and demanded a ridiculous amount for the damage to be repaired. We all chipped in and shut him up — we also returned the next evening en masse — and while some attracted his attention on one side of the store, others took a few souvenirs to balance our account. I am sure we evened the score.

Yet only a few blocks away on the same street was a café-restaurant run by a veteran of Verdun called "One-Eyed Louie." It wasn't a fancy place like the Café du Pont that had marble-topped tables, four of them, as I remember, but it was warm and "Louie" was hospitable. By now it was November, and one thing that happens in November is Thanksgiving — which, oddly enough, is something that every Frenchman knows about. It is strange that these same small-town provincials who frequently asked us such questions as "Do you perhaps know my Uncle Pierre? He works in a hotel in New York," nevertheless knew all about the Pilgrims and Thanksgiving — and, best of all, the turkey.

"*Le Dindon,*" as they call it, is not always available at the corner store in France. It certainly was not in 1917, but Louie allowed as how he could order one and cook it up for four of us and add the French fries and other fixin's for a total of two dollars a head, *vin compris.* We made a deal, and it was worth it twice over — we ate until we were ready to burst and finally quit while there was still a lot of turkey on the table. But Louie was ready with the solution to that problem. "You will come back tomorrow night — you paid for it — and I will make fresh French fried potatoes, and they will be five francs for four as always — and I will supply a bottle of wine." It was done, and Louie wiped out our peeve with the storekeeper for a while at least.

That situation didn't change much over the years. In 1925, I visited Paris on my honeymoon, and in one day I met the latter-day equivalent of the old store owner and big-hearted Louie.

It happened at that time that an epidemic of poliomyelitis had swept the world, and one of our friends was a victim — she was an eight-year-old girl, an only child, and it was a source of much sorrow. She was paralyzed from the hips down. Now, at that time there was a Viennese doctor named Lorenze who was reputed to have made miraculous cures of this dread disease — subsequently his reputation suffered, but at the moment, he was much in demand. The girl's mother was in Paris. We met, and she begged me, with my knowledge of the language, to locate Dr. Lorenze who was also visiting there.

My first step was to *Consultez le Bottin.* This book, a combination directory and phone book, is in every bar or restaurant in Paris — in fact, the owner gets a fee for having it there and displays the sign referred to above. I spotted one in a "zinc," an old-fashioned bar, as we were walking down the street together. The geography of the place was simple — the pay phone and the directory were in the rear so that anyone using it would have two chances to buy a drink — one going in another coming out. But I had other things on my mind. Having jotted down the information I needed, I was about to leave when *Monsieur le Patron* released a tirade of invective at the millionaire American who had annoyed his clients by marching in and out of his private property. He used the word *"embarrassé"* — I had obstructed and hampered his customers in my quiet and unobtrusive trip to the rear counter.

At that time, I still wore in my button hole a little piece of red and green ribbon — the colors of the *Croix de Guerre* — and I still had a fluency in French, especially the pungent words. "For this I came to France in '17?" I said. "For this I won your medal and got my nose full of gas — so I could win your gratitude and be insulted in your filthy saloon. Take your *Bottin* and shove it."

This is easily understood in both languages. Yet one hour later I entered a very prestigious jewelry store and inquired where I could have a modestly-priced necklace repaired. The clerk asked me to show him the damaged piece and took it into a back room. He returned in a few minutes with a new catch, which was the part that was broken, and refused to accept any money for the service. "After all," he said, "you and your comrades came here and liberated us from the *Sale Boche* as I see from your lapel — let me show in a small way that the French have not forgotten!"

I could guess there is much to be said on both sides, and you could probably turn the whole story around and tell it about Frenchmen in the U.S.A. I was brought to this point of view when we discussed provincialism with our interpreter, M. Levi — pronounced to rhyme with those riverside docks in New Orleans. We teased him unmercifully because the *poilus* would ask us how come we none of us spoke Spanish. Everyone had a friend or relative in Chile or Argentina, which is part of America.

Another easy way to get a rise out of most of the *simples soldats* (Buck Privates), was to pretend to read a letter from home, especially from Buffalo or Washington — the Far Western state and by association the Wild West — where we would explain those pesky Indians, *Les Peaux Rouges*, were always on the warpath.

But then one day M. Levi said, "There's good news. In the town where we stay tonight there is a good movie scheduled," and one of our latest replacements, a lad from West Virginia, said, "You mean they have movies in France?" Shades of Mellies and Pathé — our provincials are as dumb as your provincials!

If you are still interested, we never did locate Dr. Lorenze, but the youngster did improve although she never fully recovered, and, many many years later, I made another trip to France and dug out the faded ribbon and stuck it in my lapel. We rented a car and drove all over the beautiful countryside and through the bustling cities and no one noticed my decoration until we were parked outside of a famous chateau — a genuine tourist attraction — and there a bleary-eyed old codger with a two-days' growth of beard and a smell of alcohol tried to hustle me for a handout. He noticed the memento of a former glory and claimed a right of brotherhood — "I had one of those, but I had to sell it," he whined.

P.S.

He got the handout, and I hope he spent it on liquor.

CHAPTER XVII

IN CASE OF FIRE

W̶e had only been in France for a few weeks when we had a small fire. It was getting colder, and there were times when a small fire was a good thing to warm a can of beans or dry a pair of wet shoes. The trick was to heat the right product to the right temperature.

On one such occasion, a spark seems to have flown into a barracks-bag that was standing nearby. It smoldered unnoticed for some time, but the stink became obnoxious — even in the prevailing mixture of smells that encompassed drying shoes covered with mud and other detritus, plus the strong red wine on everybody's breath — and we had to put out the fire.

The results were not catastrophic — the spark and subsequent smoldering had burned holes through a suit of underwear, a shirt and a pair of britches. The owner notified the Top Sergeant, made out a list, and a couple of weeks later the burnt garments were replaced by headquarters, United States Army Ambulance Corps, Quartermaster, in Paris, France.

But, to us in SSU 592, it was a revelation. We had all seen French civilians in U.S. Army raincoats — obviously stolen from the dead or purchased from the quick, and we were anxious to obtain this additional income. We were getting $33 a month — when the paymaster showed up. But if you were caught selling your clothes, you were in trouble. And besides, if you sold them, you had nothing to wear, and it was coming on to the winter of 1917-1918. The answer was obvious — we must have a more disastrous fire and replace the clothing that had been destroyed! A very modest dilemma and easy to solve.

After a suitable lapse of time, we prepared a barracks-bag with bits and pieces of all the old cloth we could find — a blanket was torn into shirt-sized pieces, and at least one or two actual garments were included for evidence. Then, when we were quartered on the second floor of a barn, we carefully started a slow fire inside the bag and let it smolder half the night.

Then, with much "alarum" and cries of "Fire," we threw it out the door, threw hay on it to get it going strong, and then tromped it out on the cobblestone floor of the barnyard.

The results were beautiful. The courtyard was littered with charred remnants of army-issue clothing. An inventory taken the following morning, when dawn had broken, revealed a staggering loss. Recreating the totals from memory, there had been five overcoats, six pair of breaches, a dozen shirts and innumerable socks, handkerchiefs and even several blankets — all stuffed into that one barracks-bag and all burned out of recognition by this terrible conflagration.

The figures were scaled down a little bit — but the pattern was established. We received a fine load of clean, new G.I. uniforms which we sold at very reasonable prices to the French civilians — mostly storekeepers who were selling beer, wine, candy and pastry at similarly "reasonable prices."

We couldn't go to the same well for water too often, but over the next eighteen months, before we left La Belle France, we had periodic outbreaks of "fire" — which left us in funds and the local populous somewhat better-dressed!

CHAPTER XVIII

THE TONGUE SANDWICH I DIDN'T FINISH

*E*verybody has "uncles" in quotes. They are not blood rela-
tives but usually childless friends of the family who cannot be called by their first names because they are that
much older. One of mine was "Uncle Harry" — a lawyer who
did not marry until fairly late in life. At the time of World War
I, he was still a bachelor but too old for the service. He was both
a gourmet and a gourmand — as you could tell when you saw
him — and of all the people who sent me packages, his were the
most welcome. He had discovered that Fortnum & Mason, the
famous London grocers, could send almost anything to a soldier
in France, and he would have a good chance of getting it.

One such package reached me as we were moving up into
Belgium — I put it away for awhile because we were eating rather
well at that time. One of our cooks, George Thielen, was an
eccentric Texan who claimed to have been a cameraman for D.W.
Griffith. As he was over six feet tall, his statement was never
challenged. But we did know that he could cook. His father was
the leading baker of Waxahachie, Texas. In fact, George made a
birthday cake for me on June 30, 1918, when I celebrated my
nineteenth birthday, within fifty kilometers of the front lines. It
looked like a layer cake and was big enough for forty men, and he
had no flour, milk or anything else. But he cut loaves of bread in
half and laid orange slices on them over a layer of marmalade,
and it looked and tasted great.

By the time we got into action in Belgium, such nonsense
was out of the question, and we were back to "Canned Willie"

and "Goldfish," that is, corned beef and salmon — some of it from the Spanish American War. So I dug out my British goodies.

Now everybody knows about Marcel Proust and his "*madeleines*" — those delectable French pastries. In my case, the equivalent was a tongue sandwich. Throughout my youth, whenever we had cold cuts — which was quite often — there would always be plenty of ham and corned beef, but only a little tongue, for the company, because it cost the most. That made it more desirable than ever. So here was I, somewhere between Dickiebusch and Boozeboom (they are both on the map of Belgium) with a whole jar of F. & M. Potted Tongue in my *musette* (shoulder bag).

The *poste de secours* was in the cellar of what had been a fairly elaborate farm house with out-buildings and a garden with a grape arbor. Most of it was in ruins, but a few posts were still standing with vines putting out leaves and creating the illusion that it was spring here, too. It is notorious that plants grow very well in the well-fertilized soil of battlefields.

Armed with my jar of tongue, a loaf of bread and a bottle of wine, I set myself down in the arbor to have a picnic — it didn't last long.

The first shell was close enough to throw dirt on the tongue. By the time the second landed, I was underground. Obviously, the Frenchmen in charge had expected this welcome from our friends on the hills nearby — the dugout was constructed of railroad ties and was the nearest thing to bombproof I had seen. The windows — or apertures — were about eight inches high and twelve inches wide, which is just as well because through them I saw an unforgettable sight — the color of an explosion — not the smoke — but the flame. It's not funny, McGee.

Eventually, the bombardment let up, and we got customers — wounded to be evacuated. So I got into my rig and was loaded and set off for the rear, not unwillingly. I had gone about half a mile when I saw another one of our cars coming towards me. He was at least another half a mile away — this was on flat land, and the roads were all straight as a string, so visibility was excellent.

Just then a large shell exploded ahead of me. It was the kind known as a "coal bin" — it created an enormous black cloud. I stopped fast and went right into reverse — on the Model T you could do all that with your feet. I knew there was another road at right angles to this one so I took it and wasted no time leaving that place. Shells like that usually come in threes — most field artillery is in batteries of three guns. So I just left that area and got back to the main road after a detour and eventually got back to the barracks after discharging my load at the hospital.

Lo and behold, my pals were getting ready to divide my effects. The driver of the car coming towards me had seen the shell explode — and when the smoke cleared had seen no sign of my car, so he assumed I had been blown up. Obviously, he was wrong. But I still remember the taste of the tongue I never finished and my little picnic that nearly ended fatally . . . .

My other memorable gift was from "Uncle Bill" — whom I barely knew. He was an engineer for whom my mother had worked as a stenographer before the turn of the century. He never married and always jested that when "Reba" turned him down, he decided on bachelorhood. He considered me his next-of-kin. When I got into the army, he tried to find the most exotic gifts to send me. In one instance, he succeeded. He sent me a safety razor with a flashlight bulb attached — complete with a wire and a set of batteries to put in your back pocket.

The bulb was pointed at your face, and the theory was that you could shave in the dark with this tiny beam of light just where the razor met the beard. This same beam of light would serve as a perfect target for an enemy sharpshooter — unless you were indoors. But if you were indoors, even in a dugout, you would have light to shave by, and, if not, you would welcome the excuse of bad light for not shaving.

But "Uncle Bill" thought it was a great idea, and I'm sure I was the only man in the A.E.F. that had one. It came to Nancy — one-time capital of the Duchy of Lorraine — shortly after New Year, 1918. We had not been paid for two months. Our section had been detached from the XIV French Division and not yet assigned to the XVII so we were in limbo. As far as the paymaster was concerned, we didn't exist. So when I got this precious toy, my only thought was to convert it into money. Nancy was well behind the lines and had a movie theater and many cafés that were functioning. One of these was near the house in which we were quartered and was practically our other home — when we had any dough.

This particular night we had enough to get started — and with a little artificial glow, I was easily convinced to get up on one of the long tables and sell the razor. This was a big café. It held probably a hundred Frenchmen, each nursing a glass of warm beer, and I had to get their attention — and money. So first I sang two verses and three choruses of "*La Madelon*" with the naughty words — and then I asked for bids. There were none. Undaunted, my companions quickly cut up a piece of cardboard into dozens of little squares and numbered them, and we announced a raffle — at one franc a chance — to win a genuine, electrically-lighted safety razor with batteries. We sold about five chances — which didn't pay for the cardboard — then someone had an inspiration, and we added a second prize — two packs of Camel cigarettes. It was a bonanza. We sold almost 100 chances — and were cheered to the echo. I don't know who won, but I think the First Prize was exchanged for the Second Prize with two francs to boot.

Outside of that, my best gift was a package of tobacco, candy and canned fruit — except that one of the cans broke open, and I smoked the only pineapple-flavored tobacco in existence.

P.S.

The man who incorrectly reported my demise was one James Duncan Phyfe. He was a direct descendant of that early American cabinet-maker (Duncan Phyfe) who made the lyre-backed chair his trademark. During the war my folks and the Phyfes became good friends. We lived in Larchmont, and they lived in Cold Spring-on-Hudson in a house full of their great-grandfather's furniture. They called their son "Jimmy," but our Philistines naturally called him "Drunken" Phyfe, although he was reasonably abstemious.

He was slightly eccentric. The artistic genes of his ancestor impelled him to play the violin. He bought one in Nancy for fifteen hundred francs, — which at that time was the equivalent of three thousand glasses of beer! It was an old one and most likely a good buy — but the cream of the jest was that he couldn't play for sour apples. He scraped the horse hairs over those cat guts every day that we weren't actually on duty and drove us all wild — but he was such a good egg otherwise that we put up with him.

Later on I met his family and found that his father was equally odd. He was an insurance broker with offices in the Woolworth Building, like thousands of others — with one exception. He was a Sunday painter and had painted literally hundreds of canvasses — all on one subject — the White Rock girl — a nymph or naiad in a diaphanous gown posed on a rock above a spring — the trade mark for a popular brand of soft drinks. Every wall of his office had several White Rock girls, of different sizes, in an assortment of frames — but otherwise identical.

Duncan had another eccentricity — he was very trusting. He went on furlough about a month before our return to the U.S.A. By that time the American Army had taken over in force, and we ambulance drivers no longer came and went where we pleased. Dunc's train went through Lyon on the way to Nice, and he was scheduled to lay over for several hours. In the station, he "met" a girl, or she picked him up. She took him home to meet her parents and gave him her picture and promised to correspond with him. Of course, when he showed us the picture, we kidded him unmercifully — claiming to recognize her as one of the girls in Madame Louise's place on the Rue Blondell. But Duncan didn't kid — he sent for her a year later, and they were married in New York City, and Frank Kelly and I stood up for him at the wedding.

I had looked forward to the event because I hadn't spoken two words of French since my return and was eager to resume where I had left off. Of course, the first thing I asked her was, "How do you like New York?" To my surprise, she answered, "As well as ever — I was here nine years ago." That struck me as peculiar — but the ceremony was practically about to begin — so I let it go. But it came back to me later when she delivered a baby just six months after her arrival.

The French Consulate sent her back, and it was subsequently discovered that while she had not worked for Madame Louise, she had had a very lurid past including several marriages and no divorces.

Duncan recovered and moved to South Africa where he installed the giant movie screens for a famous chain of theaters. He had remarried, and I think it is in keeping with his history as outlined above that his last letter to me advised me that his wife was six months pregnant and that they had just driven through a famous national wild life preserve together and, in his own words, "What a disappointment — nary a lion did we see."

P.P.S.

By the way, Dickiebusch — a weird sort of Flemish name — stuck in our minds. Years later George Jones, of SSU 592, back home in Rutland, Vermont, married and had two children — a boy and a girl. He named the boy "Richard Bush Jones" — *Dickiebusch* to you, and the girl "Helen Lorraine Jones," because we raised *Hell in Lorraine.*

CHAPTER XIX

ON BREAD AND WINE

*I*n the previous episode, I have told how I did not get to eat a tongue sandwich near Mt. Kemmel in Belgium. But I did not mention the bread. It was French Army ration, and I loved it. It came in a round loaf about twelve inches in diameter and had a hard crust. The people who delivered it to us used a shovel to throw the rock-hard loaves off the back of a flat-bed truck as they passed the various company kitchens. The loaf was made of mixed grains — rye, barley and millet, but very little wheat, which was an item that was short in France during the Great War.

In retrospect, the American who liked the bread were the boys who learned to speak French — roughly 20% of the outfit. I suppose we were Francophiles but didn't know it. The rest never became involved in the "Polly" language — as in "Polly Vous Fransay?" — the phrase most often used to establish rapport. Without it there was no conversation and no wartime bread.

The alternative was U.S. Army white bread, which could serve as an aphrodisiac if tendered to a Mademoiselle. All the French disdained their wheatless wartime substitute. The French love bread in all its forms and gave a lot for the American version — the "wonder bread" — soft as a sofa pillow. I disdained to eat it but used it instead of money at the earliest opportunity in my 21-months' sojourn in La Belle France.

What goes with bread? Of course it's wine — a jug of it with a loaf of bread and thou. Again I speak of the French Army issue to which we were entitled. Not bottled vintage with a fancy name — this was *pinard* — a strong, red liquid with a bitter taste and a delightful after-effect. It came in cases and could be transported in a canteen or even in the spare fuel tank of an ambulance. Laced with cognac or rum, it was a lethal mixture and could be used as a paint remover. Again, those who drank it ate the issue bread and spoke French after a short time. Any conclusions you may draw from this coincidence are purely of your own making.

This brings us to beer — the alternative to wine. In Northern and Eastern France, it was not free but plentiful. We are talking of Alsace and Lorraine — the provinces that had by the end of World War I changed hands twice — and they were the home of great beer drinkers, although the province of Champagne was not far away.

The wine of that region — the old bubbly — was reserved for weddings and funerals. This Alsacian beer was a light beer — so light it was called "cat piss" and other derogatory appellations — appropriately enough, it was usually served warm. This was in a country where it was generally believed that iced drinks caused pneumonia of the stomach and were reserved for tourists on the boulevards of Paris.

One brand was called "*Bière De Maxéville*" — a suburb of Nancy. In fact, Jerry bombed the bottling plant one night when we were in residence nearby. Stupidly, we sent two ambulances to render aid and succor, but there was nobody in the plant in the middle of the night — the only casualties were the tires of the cars that rolled in broken glass from the beer bottles.

This was before Prohibition in the U.S.A., and the serious drinkers of SSU 592 who were used to Budweiser and others of that nature — strong-flavored beers — drank the French variety only as a last resort. Then, a few years passed and we got Prohibition — that monstrous mistake that created much of the gangster mentality that has prevailed ever since.

During the dreadful thirteen years that ensued, there were two or three alternatives. First, the breweries concocted a substitute product yclept "near beer." No one said how near — it had 3.4% alcohol and no taste. It was sold mainly to hospitals and penal institutions.

Next came the home brewers. It was comparatively easy to mix the mash and bottle it. Then you were supposed to put a raisin in the neck of the bottle and cork it lightly and put the results in a dark place. Some nights later, when you were entertaining the Archbishop, a series of explosions could be heard. The mash had fermented, and you now had real beer, but the bottles blew up and now you could walk in the brew, not drink it.

Finally, there were the bootleggers — usually rabbis' or clergymen's sons — who made good beer and sold it. But the mumbo-jumbo of identification and hide-and-seek that prevailed made the outcome hardly worth the trouble.

With F.D.R. came Repeal and real beer. Strangely, the speakeasies still flourished. I remember in the Fifties in Chicago going to a "speak" in the dark on a blacked-out street to buy perfectly legal beer because it gave the transaction a little romance.

Now habits have changed, and we have cholesterol and diet fads, and here came light beer — the lighter the better. The hucksters spent millions to prove which was the lightest. All they had to do was to turn back the clock to 1918 in war-torn France — and brew the beer of the time. But you would have to serve it warm!

CHAPTER XX

WITH THE BRITISH

W got involved with the British in the spring of 1918, and this is how it happened.

The war took two big turns in its fourth year — one in the spring when the Germans nearly broke the Allies' back — and the second in the fall when the "Big Parade" (as it was later called) — the massive arrival of the A.E.F. — marked the beginning of the end for "William the Lesser" (Kaiser Wilhelm II, ruler of Germany, son of Wilhelm I, who unified that frequently unhappy land).

But as late as March, 1918, nothing much had changed since our arrival the previous fall. There were attacks here and there by both sides, but experience had finally convinced the British, the French *and* the Germans that throwing in masses of men to be slaughtered would not end the war. But the Krauts had received a shot in the arm when Russia dropped out and released a lot of men for the Western Front. So, as soon as the snow melted, they gambled on knocking the Allies out before a lot of fresh American troops could get there.

This of course is ancient history now — but I bring it up because of the way it affected me. For one thing, while the British and the French were exchanging artillery fire with the Germans, they were wrangling with each other with almost as much ferocity. The argument was always how much of "The Front" each should cover, and they squabbled like neighbors who have argued over a privet hedge for generations. The Germans knew this as well as everybody else — so they attacked where the two armies joined or failed to join because each said the other was supposed to be farther west or east.

This was the Battle of the Somme, and it was touch and go all through the spring of 1918. The British 5th Army caught the brunt of it, and they backed up rather rapidly. Our own Irishman, John Green, was heard to remark that the Limies had put their running shoes on. But it was easier to criticize before we saw what they were up against.

Our own division, the XIV French, was still in Lorraine — not many miles from our first "front," but a lot livelier. There was no more Gentlemen's Agreement about shelling a couple of empty lots every afternoon at five. But it still wasn't total war. So when the British ran into trouble farther west, our division — among others — was sent to fill the gap in the lines.

We traveled by freight train for two nights and three days, and it was quite a trip. To begin with, we finally learned first hand about the legend of the "40 or 8" that was stenciled on every French box car. (The American Legion named their "fun loving" section after this insignia, but they called it the "40 *and* 8" — which was a misnomer. It was bad enough in the correct version — 40 men *or* 8 horses.)

Every freight car or side-door Pullman had four iron rings bolted to the wall at each end. This was to tether four horses — each set of four facing in the opposite direction and between the two quartets their grooms — the unfortunate artillerymen or cavalrymen (they still had those in 1918) could recline at leisure between eight pairs of flying hooves because the horses didn't like to ride in box cars. The rest of the troops had no horses to contend with — every forty men had a whole car to themselves. And remember, these cars were less than half the size of an American freight car.

We were only 35, but they let us have a whole car. You could choose your resting place. The floor was lined with hay. If you went to either end, you could suffocate quietly. In the middle section, you could enjoy the view and the night air and easily roll out the open door. Needless to say, there were some who voted to close the doors and others violently opposed. All told, it made for a wild ride.

We started off going due south — with a mixture of flat cars on which our ambulances had been bolted down and box cars for our occupancy, as described above. Because of the compass direction, we immediately decided we were going to Italy — where the retreat at Caporetto was in full swing. This is the battle that Ernest Hemingway immortalized in *A Farewell to Arms*. He was in that battle, too, and as an ambulance driver.

One of his buddies was Adolph Menjou who trained with us at Allentown and eventually became a movie star and acted in the picture they made out of the book — only he became the Italian liaison officer when he actually had been the American Lieutenant in charge of ambulances. (Menjou also starred as an evil, sadistic French General, along with Kirk Douglas, in another great movie about World War I — "Paths of Glory.")

I have some vivid memories of Adolph from Camp Crane. He made Officers Training Corps and, as I said, ended up with an ambulance outfit in Italy. Much later, he wrote a pretty good book, *Nine Tailors Make A Man*. Louis Hirschkorn saw him autographing copies at a department store in Washington, D.C. Louis said, "Dolph! Why don't you come to a USAAC meeting? You know we have a great organization." Menjou rebuffed him, uttering sentiments that he despised the USAACs. But by that time he had become a near-fascist and disdained his connection with the Florence Nightingale side of his and my service in the USAAC of World War I.

But we didn't go to Italy. After a few hours of hurtling through the countryside at about 15 miles an hour, we turned west and began to make a great half circle from Lorraine to Paris — all of 150 miles as the crow flies, but it took us 48 hours and we covered about 500 miles.

The first night out we were awakened about 2 a.m., much to our disgust, because we had stopped in a station where the French Red Cross ladies were dishing out coffee. But our anger was short-lived. The coffee was heavily laced with rum — the combination is known as "*l'anyol*," in the argot of the *poilu*, and it is truly a potent beverage and panacea for all ills. Suddenly the straw grew softer — the rhythm of the wheels became more musical — and we slept through most of Burgundy.

In the morning, we discovered that there were little cabins on the roof of every third or fourth car where a trainmen could operate a set of brakes when trains were being assembled. These now became our observation posts, and we played switchman, engineer and brakeman in a haze of rum and a warm spring day in France — just about the greatest combination you can get!

In the late afternoon, we entered the *Ceinture*, the belt of tracks that runs around Paris so that trains coming from any direction can leave in any other direction within 180° of circumference. It's not that easy. We backed and forthed and lost our engine and got a new one, and at one point in a freight yard on the outskirts of the "City of Light," we were solicited by a couple of girls who offered to service us through a wire fence that separated us from them. No one accepted their offer, but it did have a fascination — depending so much on the size of the mesh in the wire.

But we left Paris shortly and wandered around another night and finally detrained at a place called "*Creil.*" I wrote it down then, as I took note of most of the places we stopped in — and half a century later I learned that it was the site of a famous pottery during the Empire. A good friend of mine imported a modern version of "*Creil*" as recently as the 60s by which time I had gone into the pottery business myself.

We had now reached the boundary where the British took over although for the moment the situation was fluid — very fluid. The French and the British were sharing the discomforts of a badly- organized alliance, and it was just about this time that Marshall Foch was named Supreme Commander, the whole deck was reshuffled, and most likely the war was won then and there. But all we knew was that the men with whom we were living and working spoke a different language — not only different from the inhabitants but different from ours as well.

The Tommies had been there for four years. Some of them were actually "Mons" men — having fought at the Battle of Mons in 1914 (where, allegedly, a vision of angels had been vouchsafed to the British troops) — whom the Germans called the "Contemptibles," and they liked that name and kept it. But in all those four years they never learned the "Polly" language ("*Parlez-vous français?*"). They did have some expressions that bore translation, such as "Napoo" — meaning, "There ain't any more." (In French, "*Il n'y en a plus,*") and, believe it or not — "simperium" — meaning, "It makes no difference." (In French, "*Ça ne fait rien.*") Of course, this was one big reason why they didn't get along any better, and it went right through the British Army from top to bottom. There are vestiges of the same feeling in Canada to this day — mutual misunderstanding is the name of that game.

They were pretty good to us — in a British way. They did think we were a long time coming — which was true from their point of view. But they didn't fraternize the way Americans are wont to do. If you asked for something to eat, you got it. But it wasn't offered. I have stood warming myself before a fire on which the Tommies were toasting bread on bayonets — which is very bad for the steel — and I could have starved if I hadn't swallowed my pride and said, "How about a piece of that." To use their own expression, they were a "rum lot." When a fight broke out, which was frequently, they would form a ring and take sides. The colloquy would go:

"Who's down now?" "Why, that's our Tim." "Well, let him up — fair play — you know." "And who's down now?" "The other fellow." "Well kick 'im. Boot 'im. Give 'im the leather."

And so forth.

We were told at once to avoid the Manchester regiments as they would rob you blind. But they were all light-fingered — they invented "liberating" property long before the word was popular. We lost everything that wasn't bolted to the cars — but it only took us a few days to catch on. Then we took pen knives and cut short sticks from bushes. With a stick under your arm, you became an officer — the British carried swagger sticks, remember. And then we just commandeered what we required. We would drive up to a supply dump on the way back from unloading at a base hospital and get a can or two of lubricating oil, legally, and fill the car with bacon and marmalade, by flourishing our officers' insignia.

One memory stands out above all the rest — the ritual of the bath. Every so often, the quiet of the morning would be broken by a military band — and here would come the fifes and drums with the drum major resplendent in a "shako" extending his six feet to seven — and back of all this splendor and pomp would appear forty or fifty Tommies in shirt sleeves, each with a towel

over one shoulder. They were sheep being led to the slaughter —
or British going to the baths.

So we passed about three weeks in the British sector without
really penetrating the British way of facing the world. One
Tommy summed it up this way, "You say we're unfriendly —
what nonsense — here's my pal and him and me have been like
brothers for twenty years — ain't that friendly?" As they say in
printing — "stet."

I would like to insert a serious note before leaving for
Belgium — which we did, in May. Nobody has ever gone deeply
into our motivations or those of the other Allies — or the enemy
for that matter. We were mostly youngsters who believed in Mr.
Wilson — we were going to make the world safe for democracy.
Remember, we were enlisted men — before the draft began. The
French were fighting for their lives, and they knew it. Even the
right wing socialists wanted to win the war — and then overturn
the capitalist system.

But the poor bloody British didn't know why the hell they
were there, and whatever they were told by their superiors — the
Oxford and Cambridge crowd — they took it with a grain of salt
— or more likely a pound of it. In my opinion, that's why they
didn't do so well. I'm still a believer in dedication to causes and
its result in meeting the enemy — physical or otherwise.

CHAPTER XXI

IN BRAVE LITTLE BELGIUM

*I*n April of 1918, we had come by train to the area of the Somme, where our French division was supposed to go into the gap which the enemy had made between the British and French armies. For all I know, they did just that. But we were never involved. Instead, we were moved around back of the lines in every compass direction, day by day, occasionally evacuating French, British and even Italian wounded men — the Allies had thrown everything into the area.

Finally, as April gave way to May, we went further north and west and crossed the border into Belgium, and here our division was committed to a holding action opposing Mt. Kemmel, and we went on duty for our most strenuous campaign so far. In a period of eighteen days — May 12 to 30 — all twenty of our cars were on duty in twelve-hour shifts and some right around the clock. We had a considerable number of minor casualties, mostly gas cases, and, in retrospect, I think we all had a bit of "battle fatigue" or "shell shock."

But before we got that far, we spent a few days in the Belgian "rear" while our division was preparing to take over from the British — not a simple matter at any point, but most difficult in full view of the enemy. This was and is flat land — reasonably fertile but not physically attractive. As I said before, the inhabitants had early discovered that a straight line is the shortest distance between two points — so they built their roads like city streets in a vast gridiron — great for fast communication in peace time but very rough when under fire because your enemy gunner could drop his eggs at the crossroads and save a lot of gunpowder.

In this case, he was further aided by the fact that he was looking down our necks from a ridge of hills which runs across the southern half of that country properly known as the Kingdom of the Belgians.

This small unit in the old European set-up of continually squabbling nation-states is still further divided between Flemish and Walloons — who are mutually antipathetic and speak different languages.

Flemish is the language of Flanders and is close to Dutch. The Walloons speak French — with perhaps a little local accent. But the paradox is that the Flemish are alongside the French border, at least the part near the sea, so that Flanders Fields, where the poppies grow, is where you land if you are coming to the aid of the Brave Little Belgian Army. This was true in 1914 and was still true in 1918. (And was even still true, by the way, in 1939.)

Our first Belgian billet was on a farm near the French border city of Arques. We knew we were there when the owner started shrieking at us in Flemish. Except for the volume, which she kept high at all times, it sounded like Pennsylvania Dutch, which we had sampled a few months before — a lifetime really — in Allentown, Pennsylvania.

Madame X, our first Belgian contact, was running a farm and substituting for all the men that had gone to war — and doing quite well, thank you. Years before Women's Lib was heard of, she ruled the roost with an iron hand. To begin with, the well was padlocked, and we paid for our drinking water. After nearly four years of propaganda about Poor Little Belgium, this was quite a shock. But Madame stuck to her rights. According to her story, the English had paid for their water, the French ditto, and if the Germans came the next day, they would pay, too. So the Americans paid in their turn.

She sold sugar, too, in bags marked "Gift of the Grateful American People." But that wasn't surprising — we had gotten accustomed to it after buying cigarettes similarly marked in many places. She did have one unique qualification — a son about fifteen named for a hero of antiquity, Aeneas, the protagonist of Virgil's *Aeneid*, whom a few of us had met just one year before in the ivy-covered halls of our colleges. This one was a lout of a boy who was studying for a career in the army by getting lost at every opportunity to avoid work in any form. His mother knew his tricks and pursued him relentlessly. Her cries of "Aeneas — Aeneas," rang out at all hours, and for a touch of humor in a drab existence (ours), she pronounced it "IN - E - ASS." We needed the comic relief.

It rained most of the time. It was April — month of showers — and there was a theory that all that cannon firing had loosened up the water works. I heard that same theory in 1958 at the World's Fair in Brussels — only then it was the H-Bomb that was being tested in the Pacific. The point is that it always rains in Belgium — only sometimes more than others. The British had been living in it for three years. They had made a whole province of trenches — first line, second line, third line and communication trenches lined with duck boards to keep their feet dry — but you couldn't drive a Ford in them — so we sashayed back and forth on top feeling conspicuous, with those nice bright red crosses on a white ground serving as targets.

We were not the only ones on top of the ground. There was plenty of artillery and caissons and trucks, but by this time they were "camouflaged." We had only recently heard the word and seen the product. Some of it was spectacular. In Lorraine, the French had a little ammunition train painted to resemble a picket fence — only it had to be standing still to fool anybody. But they did do green and brown mixtures that looked like trees and bushes and did blend into the countryside where there was still some foliage to blend into.

In Belgium it was almost barren after so much cannonading

back and forth so everything stuck out like a sore thumb. On top of that the British, intransigent as usual, had mostly contempt for "camouflage" — a French word to begin with. They took the pots of paint that were issued to them and painted "To Hell With The Kaiser" on their tents — or a nose with a thumb and four fingers extended in His Majesty's general direction. I don't know how they looked from the air — Jerry did have spotter planes — but at this late date in the war, it appears that they may have done as much good as a pastoral after Watteau painted on a pup tent. One thing is sure, in camp we felt like a man walking down the street bearing a sign saying "Kick Me."

Somewhere along the line one of our boys ran over a pig — or, to be more exact, a sow. The animal had darted across the road in front of him. The driver was blameless but guilty just the same. He reported it and forgot about it. Almost exactly one year later — as we were preparing to embark on a transport to return to our homeland — he was summoned to a board of inquiry concerned with the recompense that the Belgian farmer was claiming from the American government. It seems the sow was pregnant, and the canny Belgian (they are the Scotch of the Continent) wanted the U.S. to pay for the unborn litter. Frank Kelly, the culprit, a fine upstanding Irish lad from Ossining, New York, answered all the questions freely until they asked in which compass direction the pig was headed. Then he told them what to do with the pig — a difficult task involving still another pig.

But this was a soggy interlude before the main event. At Reninghelst we caught up with the war. We were in convoy, proceeding in an orderly fashion in a line of trucks, wagons, guns, caissons, etc., when hell started to pop at the crossroads we were approaching. We had no place to go but dismounted and made ourselves inconspicuous in the ditch that ran alongside the road. It was over in a few minutes, and we were none the worse for it, but just up ahead, a city block away, they were clearing the remains of some fine-looking Scotch Highlanders — six footers all of them — who had been maintaining traffic at the juncture.

Our spirits were much dampened by this experience, and we were not encouraged when we were encamped directly in front of a battery of very large guns that fired over our heads and damn near blew the roofs off of our Ford ambulances and murdered sleep more completely than Macbeth. Surprisingly, some top brass saw that this was a bad situation, and we were moved about a mile and quartered in a reasonably clean, wooden barracks that had been British for three years when this area was well behind the lines.

It was still comparatively quiet, with desultory shelling at the crossroads, when we were escorted to our *postes de secours*. All four (one for each regiment in the division) were four or five kilometers from H.O.E. (Hospital of Evacuation — so designated by the English initials and pronounced in the French fashion "Ash-Oh-A"). This necessitated a relay system of four more cars roughly half way out — to replace the cars coming in loaded — then a third set of four cars at the base would move into position as they do in baseball. So you were either "at bat," "on deck" or "in the hole" at most times. As we had twenty cars and this schedule called for twelve, you can calculate on your fingers and toes that we were short from the start.

Then we had breakdowns — real and imaginary. It may come as a shock, but Americans are no more courageous than any other people. We are all capable of great deeds of derring-do, and we all have a nice yellow streak somewhere along the spine — only some are wider than others. So it was not unusual for a car to go out and come back almost immediately because the brakes or steering were not working properly, which would necessitate a delay before the driver had to face a definitely dangerous trip to the Front. One such occurrence by a driver, who shall remain nameless, prompted our mechanic, John Greene, to quip, "I fixed him up, but he'll be back in a little while to say he forgot his handkerchief."

In many cases, an element of prudence entered into our calculations. For example, shelling came in bursts of ten or fifteen minutes — during which you could pop into a dugout and wait for the storm to subside. Jerry obviously didn't have an inexhaustible supply of ammo, and guns have to be re-bored after they've been fired a certain number of times, so you could lower the risk of being hit by trying to travel between the outbursts.

On two such occasions, I found myself in the dugout at the midway station. In one case, my relief was a carefree lad (Lawrence Whitney Collins) of fine lineage with an excellent palate for fine wines and spirits. He calmed my fears and sent me on my way by telling me a long, involved story about his girlfriend who had been photographed wearing a gob's hat, under the misapprehension, she claimed, that her "Larry" was in the Navy. After that it seemed ridiculous to worry about a few shells.

The second incident was quite different. This time my buddy explained very carefully that he was half owner of a large textile mill in Reading, Pennsylvania, and was certain that in case of his demise his partner would grab the other half. His conclusion was to wait another half hour before proceeding to the first aid station — on the oft-repeated belief, "You won't win the war today — take your time."

The most amazing reaction came from a man who was our greatest crap-shooter. He could shoot for a thousand francs without batting an eyelid. But he developed more illnesses and his car had the most problems of any, during our three weeks in that place. And the one man who never missed his turn and did two men's work without a word was Charley Walker from Seattle, known as "Kerensky" because he was big and blond. Many months later, Kerensky got in a crap game, and when he had won about a hundred bucks, he was so nervous that two of us had to help him hide the money and take him away from the game. (It's true that this was on the transport ship coming home, and his opponents were the U.S. Navy boys, who were not good losers.)

I kept a pink sheet from that tour of duty — it was called a *livret matricule* — and you listed the time and the number of cases you carried *assis* (sitting) or *couchés* (lying down). Our cars carried four sitting up on two little benches that folded down from the sides or three lying down on stretchers — two on the floor and the third suspended on straps about half way from the floor to the roof. I am not being funny when I say that the trick was to keep the bleeders out of that upper section.

Anyway, my book shows that I carried a total of 230 men — all French by that time — in a 36-hour period. (I had some rest in between.) That indicates that our section probably evacuated a total of 4 or 5 thousand before the division was relieved.

It was a great performance for 35 untrained men in a strange country. Our first-aid drill did us no good, and the Number One Man never knew which end of the stretcher he should lift. But we did perform. On the way out we felt relieved — to put it mildly — and most of us took off the tin hats that we had been wearing 'round the clock and put on our comfortable "louse cages" — the overseas cap that had replaced our beloved Stetsons. But we were still in the war zone, and the order came to halt the convoy and fall-in in formation.

We had a brand-new interpreter — book-taught and not too well taught. He explained that we should still wear proper equipment — and closed with the remark, "And now you will put on your casques and climb into your chariots — isn't it?" (*"n'est-ce pas"* — "isn't that so" ends every second sentence in French conversation.) He was answered by a beautiful raspberry — or Bronx cheer — and our French Lieutenant, descended from a

147

marquis of the *ancien regime,* took it personally. Result, we were not mentioned in orders, that is, "cited" to the divisional head-quarters, and we did not receive the *Fouragères* of the Croix-de-Guerre — a sort of telephone cord in green and red that is worn on the left shoulder.

As you know, a few individuals were cited and did get the medal, including *moi* .

CHAPTER XXII

Greaseless Greeman

*A*s I have explained, during the fall of 1917 and the winter that followed, we were attached to the XIV Division of the French Army. This was a so-called "territorial" division — we would have called them "Home Guards." They were all old men — not only fathers but grandfathers. They were fine examples of why the French soldiers were called *poilus*. They were not just hairy — they were bearded almost to a man — and most of the beards were gray, if not white. A good insight into the nature of these warriors was their everyday speech, especially their cuss words, which ran along the lines of "*Sacré bleu!*" (roughly translated "Good Heavens") or the famous "*Nom d'une pipe!*" (which can't be translated at all).

After a reasonable period in the trenches, where the most dangerous spots are well marked with signs — "KEEP YOUR HEAD DOWN HERE" or "*EN PLEINE VUE DE L'ENNEMI*" — each regiment would be withdrawn for a period of *repos* and replaced by more of the same guardians of their country. The most serious case we had in sixty days was a guy who nearly cut his leg off chopping wood while in his cups.

The replacement of one group by another extended to the medics. The Captain and a couple of Lieutenants in charge of a *poste de secours* would pack up their bags of personal odds and ends — including sweaters, books, cards and even phonographs, and an ambulance — one of ours — would take him to the rear while a new set moved in the dugouts which had become subterranean apartments over three years of the stalemate. Everything was done with all the protocol of a diplomatic détente as those

departing explained to the new arrivals where the most comfortable accommodations could be found and which stove gave the
most heat. It was a hell of a way to win a war — and the proof is
that they weren't winning it.

The spring of 1918 changed all that — for us as well as for
thousands of others. When your outfit was pulling back, you
didn't stop for niceties. You met your relief and wished them
luck, and that was that. The slogan of the day was "*Sauve qui
peut!*" or "Every man for himself!" on a shelled road.

Then came the summer of 1918 and lots more changes. The
nature of the War changed along about July 14th — Bastille Day
— when a big German attack was repulsed, and the last threat to
Paris was ended at Château-Thierry. Meanwhile, we were attached
to a new division, the XVII, and they were a different breed of cat.
A lot younger and tougher, their favorite epithet would be along
the line of a "*Mille Putains de Bordel de Dieu*" (that's "A Thousand
Whores from the Brothel of God"), and that was just for openers.
We didn't have any more drunks chopping wood, but we did have
plenty of stretcher cases to fill our ambulances going to the rear
night and day and then going up for more.

Of course, these troops had to be relieved, the same as our
old buddies, and so there came a day when we got a call at headquarters to send a car to a certain place to pick up a Captain and
a couple of Lieutenants who were being relieved for a much-
needed rest. Now this was not quite the same as the old time
"moving day" that I have described. This meant driving an extra
trip to a definitely unpleasant place to bring back unwounded
men. Incidentally, it was not according to Hoyle. The Geneva
Convention or its equivalent said ambulances were for wounded
only, but nobody paid any attention to that except me. It was
my turn to go, and I had been working for about eighteen hours,
and I thought they should have sent a staff car.

But I didn't do anything about it. I cranked up and took off
— leaving a trail of sulphurous remarks behind me. Nor did I
stop to check gas, oil or anything else. That was a mistake. I had
gone about five miles when my motor quit. When I went to start
it, I couldn't even turn the crank. And when I tried to push it off
the road, I couldn't even turn the rear wheels — with the brakes
off and four friendly French *soldats* to help.

Although I am not now and never have been a mechanic, I
knew enough to diagnose this ailment. I had burned out the
motor and the differential because both were bone dry — lacking
in lubricant and, to use a technical phrase, "frozen solid."

At this time I was in the remnants of a little town, and there
was a command post with field telephones. I got in touch with
my outfit — a replacement was sent to bring back the staff at the
outpost, and a tow truck was dispatched for my wagon.

The truck came in a in few minutes, and I was towed in igno-
miniously — with only my front wheels on the ground and my
hind end in the air. Arriving at our quarters, I was lowered,
unhooked and prepared to abandon ship. But I reckoned without
my host. Among the changes that summer had brought was a new
commanding officer. Lieutenant Harding was a tall, good-looking
"90-Day Wonder" — nothing like "Doctor" Lieutenant Mauser,
our original Daddy, nor yet like our own Lieutenant Smith, who
had been a Sergeant of the Amherst section. This man was from
transportation — as the Army had finally figured out that we really
had nothing to do with the Medical Corps. We were not descendants of Florence Nightingale but more nearly related to Louis
Chevrolet — a racing driver of the period who gave his name to a
fairly well known product of General Motors. (Years later, someone found out that his widow was driving a Ford.)

So here was my pleasant, but firm, young officer asking me if
I had checked my oil and grease. I answered — without hesita-

tion and in the affirmative. I even remembered the day and the hour and that for me was a matter of pride that I never failed to keep track of such essentials.

Alas, my act was not good enough. To my surprise, he got down in the mud in his brand-new whipcord breeches and put his hand on the rear housing. He took it away, fast. It was still hot — proof conclusive of my guilt. I was told to report after roll call the following morning.

The meeting was short and sweet. The Lieutenant told me what I already knew — that I was guilty of a Court Martial Offense — Carelessly Destroying Government Property — to wit, the mechanical part of an ambulance — and at a time when they were in great demand and short supply. In fact, this was my second that month — the other having been destroyed by hostile shellfire.

For once, I was without an answer. But the Fates were on my side. The new commander was not anxious to have a court martial on his record. So he offered me Company Punishment at my discretion. I accepted with alacrity. I got thirty days in the kitchen as K.P. (the infamous "Kitchen Police"), so I peeled a few hundred potatoes and ate a great many of them plus a few steaks and other goodies which the cooks always managed to extract from the supplies before the bulk of it was rendered inedible be our "Goulash Cannon" — the rolling kitchen.

To this day, if I have any small ability at whipping up a tasty dinner at short notice, I owe it all to Lieutenant Harding and "Buck" Miller and George Thielen, our two cooks. We thought their food was pretty bad — until we lost them. But I knew they were in a class with Brillat-Savarin when you shared your liquor with them.

There is only one footnote. I was inspired to write a poem commemorating my fall from Grace. I called it "Greaseless Greeman" and sent it in to *Stars and Stripes* — official gazette of the A.E.F. To my surprise, they published it, but if I ever had a copy, I mislaid it long ago. All I remember is that I rhymed "Differential" with "Essential" but had trouble with "Magneto."

In a later war, at a later date, I would have coupled "Carburation" and "Fornication" and might have made *Esquire* magazine.

Complete with mustache, Croix de Guerre and German "Gott Mit Uns" belt buckle. (Hemingway wore one just like it.)

CHAPTER XXIII

Veux-Tu Baiser La Patronne?

I was asked this question sometime in June, 1918, just before my 19th birthday. SSU 592 had been taken out of action because the division to which we were attached, the XIV French Infantry Division, had suffered considerable casualties in Belgium during May and needed replacements.

We were quartered on a farm in Milly-sur-Terrain, a lovely name for a peaceful village "somewhere in France," as the censors put it. The ambulances were lined up in the courtyard on a farm, and the men were quartered in the barn. For sleeping, there was a choice between the hayloft or the cars. The former was warmer, but the hay or straw would probably have small animals within that could penetrate sleeping bags or mattresses which were themselves straw-lined. The cars had stretchers that had been sterilized, after a fashion, following each use, but they were comparatively hard and narrow. At any rate, I chose the stretcher but mitigated the discomfort by piling on three or four good, thick blankets, which I had thoughtfully stolen from various hospitals over the preceding days.

After evening chow, we didn't waste much time before "corking off" — a slang phrase, long since forgotten, for sleep, "that knits up the raveled sleave of care," in this case a natural fatigue after a month opposite Mt. Kemmel, a highly concentrated base for German artillery. Dusk had fallen when a French soldier attached to our unit — I think he was a mechanic or maybe a cook's helper — opened the flap of my Ford and posed the question which is the title of this chapter.

At this point, I must explain — for my readers who are not linguists — that the French language has some peculiarities. The noun "*le baiser*" is the kiss, as famed in song and story. You can give or receive a kiss (*un baiser*), but the verb is another matter. It means to have sexual intercourse. You don't "*baiser*" your mother or father — unless you are a very strange person, indeed — you embrace them (*embrasser*). So my friend's question was, to put it bluntly, "How would you like to fuck the old lady?"

I had seen her earlier in the day, and she wasn't that old — maybe forty — just about twice my age. She was simply but tastefully attired in a black *jupon* (apron) with a blouse to match — suitable for milking cows, pitchforking manure or other chores that descended on so many Frenchwomen whose husbands were "at the Front," if not already casualties, in 1918. So I agreed, and, after a short interval, she climbed in, and I climbed on.

It was not a love match and bore little resemblance to the amorous dalliance for which Frenchwomen are famous. But she was satisfied, and so was I, and neither of us had any qualms or afterthoughts. In fact, in the morning, when we moved out, all in the same uniform, I doubt if she recognized me.

Today, I am told, such brief jousts on the field of love are very common. My own, over seventy years later, is just a memory.

CHAPTER XXIV

PANCAKES ON THE MARNE

*A*lmost everyone in my outfit was a "character" — what the French call "*un type.*" One of the most predictable was George F. Jones — a Vermont Yankee who could be counted on to react in true Green Mountain style in almost any set of circumstances. One such reaction saved three lives, including his own.

George was not a farm boy. He was born and brought up in Rutland, the metropolis of his natal state. But the truth is that Rutland was only one short main street of shops and banks, and half a mile away you would be in open country. This was certainly the case in the early years of the century when George and growing up. It was then that he acquired the habit of getting up at 6 a.m. and putting away a stack of wheat cakes plentifully anointed with maple syrup — the local nectar. He had lacked both these dainties for a long while, but he still got up at 6 a.m., and that is the point of this story.

By October of 1918, the Allied Armies in France were advancing rapidly, and the German Army was retreating. But the retreat was not a rout. It was not precipitous, and they still threw a lot of iron and steel at the conquerors, who didn't feel very sure of the future. They had been in the relative security of the trenches for a long while, and now were out in the open and felt naked.

Personally I shared this feeling as I drove my ambulance over roads that still had German signs on them and slept in dugouts that had recently known the smell of sauerkraut. These dugouts were quite a sight. They had been occupied with little change for four years — the early, hand-dug versions with a few sandbags had gradually been deepened, enlarged and covered with concrete. Not only that. They were electrically lighted, ventilated and heated. In many cases, they were elaborately decorated — with French *meubles* (furniture) that had been liberated during their conquering march in 1914.

One of these deserves a mention. Some wild young knaves had pillaged a curtain and drapery store along the way, and their dugout was tastefully hung with at least fifty yards of pink satin — giving it all the ambiance of a well-run whorehouse. There was one drawback to these luxury dwellings — the entrances and exits slanted the wrong way. Naturally, the Germans built them so that the danger of a stray shell dropping in was very slight and opposite to its trajectory if fired from our side. Now a German shell could pop in and ruin everybody's comfort if the artilleryman got lucky.

On the night of which I write, about October 20, we had departed from our regular routine of sending one car to each of the four regimental first aid stations — because we were moving pretty fast. We sent all four to a kind of midway point — still well behind the front lines — with the idea of splitting them up and dispatching them to their ultimate destination the following morning. On arrival, we had a well-cooked meal prepared on the very elaborate stove that our German cousins had left behind. There was even Danish butter in the cans which we had been told not to eat lest it be poisoned. P.S. — it was delicious.

After eating, we prepared to bed down in the nice warm smelly *abri* (dugout) in a good, thick haze of tobacco smoke. But George, the country boy, would have none of it. He insisted on sleeping in his car — on a nice, clean stretcher smelling slightly of disinfectant. And he proceeded to con the rest of us into his way of thinking. It was a beautiful night, not really cold, and we had plenty of blankets. As far as our safety was concerned, George pointed out that the chance of enemy fire was very slight, and if a shell did come over, it could go right down the stairs and kill everybody in the hole — while upstairs the chances were mathematically in our favor with all the open country around us. He won the argument. He usually did. His father and an older brother were lawyers and later state's attorneys, and George much later became judge of the probate court. So we all slept in our wagons.

Promptly at 6 a.m., George woke up and smelled coffee cooking — the damn dugout had a chimney, no less — and nothing would do but we must all go down to breakfast and with our combined French vocabulary talk the Frogs into making pancakes. Grumbling, we complied. But those pancakes never got made. Within minutes it grew light and our four light-green Fords — with nice red crosses on a white ground — were just too tempting. Somebody on the other side was sore because the Kaiser had lied to him, among other things, and he yanked the cord and sent just one 88 millimeter (diameter) shell in our direction.

Avoiding the open door of the shelter, it landed squarely on George's ambulance and ruined it. It was H.E. (high explosive) — the kind that doesn't make a big hole but sends pieces of flying shrapnel in all directions. All four of the cars had holes in them at various levels — and we argued for quite a while as to who would have been hit and where. But George was our overnight hero with his Country Boy habits.

About six weeks later, after the Armistice, we were in a real small town by the name of Cumières, on the Marne, about fifty kilometers east of Château-Thierry where the first turn-around really started. There was not a restaurant in Cumières — not even a proper café — the place couldn't support one. But there were two or three *estaminets*. This is a cross between a store and a café-restaurant — in addition to being the home of the proprietor. And it was in such a place that George determined to have his pancakes.

159

George's French was not too good. He had, besides, a slight speech defect — he mumbled a little and spattered his listeners occasionally. In fact, he was known as "old marble mouth" — a subtle tribute to Demosthenes and also to the principal export product of Vermont — after maple syrup.

He started slowly by conveying by word and gesture that he was ready to eat. Madame was willing and anxious to please. So George started off with eggs (*oeufs*) accompanied by cackling sounds and then milk (*du lait*) with an appropriate "moo" — "*Mais oui monsieur, une omelette, n'est-ce pas?*"

"No, damn it, not an omelet," said our hero — and began making flat circular motions with his hands until Madame said — "*Phonographe?*" — but then quickly correcting herself. Just as George was adding a pinch of salt, she suddenly seemed to be catching on.

"*Venez avec moi,*" she said, catching his sleeve — and proceeded to lead him from the store through its back door into her kitchen, and thence to her living room, and finally to the bedroom, with its great, big bed covered with quilts and spreads. Now she got down on her hands and knees and pulled George down beside her. She put one hand under the bed, cried "*Voila!*" and drew forth what do you think — a large platter of pancakes!

The explanation is simple — these were what the French call "*crêpes.*" They are sour milk pancakes that are made in advance and later served with jam or other filling and, in their most elaborate form, with orange juice, butter and brandy — as *crêpes suzettes*.

Normally, a restaurant would have a supply of them in the refrigerator. But our *patronne* didn't own one, so she kept them in the coolest place in the house — on the stone floor, under the bed.

For once the story has a happy ending — George ate two helpings, and we all found the place and ate many variations on the theme, substituting grenadine syrup for maple syrup and telling the story to all who would listen — that many good things can be found under the bed.

CHAPTER XXV

THE BIG PARADE AS SEEN FROM A SMALL HOLE

OR

A BIRD'S-EYE VIEW OF WAR — FROM THE GROUND

*I*t is a truism that you cannot see the forest on account of the trees. This is particularly true of a modern war. No soldier knows he is in the Second Battle of the Marne until he reads it in the newspapers some time later. But there are times when everyone, down to the lowest Buck Private, knows that things are happening. In my own experience, from September, 1917, until March, 1918, it was obvious that nothing was happening. In fact, anyone caught firing a gun at the enemy was promptly put down — nobody wanted to make waves. Then, from March until July of 1918, we were moving backward — which you could see on the map — because we were getting closer to Paris and further from Berlin from day to day. In July and August, we were too busy to stick pins in maps — but, in September, something significant happened.

Our outfit, attached to the XVII French Division of Infantry, was several miles behind the lines for regrouping. At about 8 p.m., on September 26, right after dark, we began to a hear a lot of cannon fire — on our side. It increased until by midnight the sky was lit up as far as the eye could reach both to the left and right — that is, west and east of our encampment. It kept up all night and 24 hours later we moved — and we moved north. We came to places that had been in German hands for nearly four years — and for the first time we began to think that we would win the war — and it would not take four more years.

Until then, a popular joke ran like this. First man — "How long are you in for?" Second Man — "Three years more." First man — "Lucky you — I'm in for the duration."

After all, we had heard French soldiers say "We're licked, let's call it a day — and go home." But that's another story. Anyway we were moving, and each day we would take off at about 5 p.m. to a new poste de secours (each regiment had one — and as a French division has four regiments — that means that four ambulances went on duty every evening to relieve the previous crews).

So on or about October 1, I drove off with fairly complete instructions as to where I was going. We found our way by looking for stakes driven into the edge of the road with the number of the regiment and a spade, heart, diamond or club painted on it. All four of our regiments had been cited for bravery — or foolhardiness — and been awarded the *Fouragère* of the *Croix de Guerre* — a green and red cord worn around the shoulder. This made the XVII a division of "aces" hence the hearts, spades, etc.

This was a lovely day as October days can be. The front lines had moved so fast that we were in relatively untouched terrain. Also it was rolling country, not heavily wooded — typical farm land. I came to a rise in this road and found my marker and also a sign left from more peaceful days "Moulin de Perthes." So I looked for the mill. I found part of it. It had been a wooden windmill such as Don Quixote may have attacked — there are still some in Holland. None of the superstructure was standing — it had probably been destroyed early in the war — but the base was intact — a circular opening about 15 feet across with a cast iron rim on which the whole thing turned when the wind veered.

The hole had probably been deeper but the sides had caved in so I found a ready-made observation post from which I could survey the countryside. Nothing loath, I abandoned my errand of mercy to take a look-see. I had long since lost all resemblance to Florence Nightingale and operated my "meat wagon" as we affectionately dubbed our *voitures sanitaires* on a schedule guaranteed to allow me an occasional coffee break or something more stimulating.

As I stood in this cellar of the old mill with my head just barely sticking out, I saw a marvelous little drama. Down the road I had taken came a battery of French 75's — the famous *soixante-quinze* now immortalized as a particularly potent cocktail. They were horse drawn — two teams to a gun and two more to the fourgon — the ammunition wagon. They turned into the field below me, debouched into a line and in a few minutes had set up the traditional battery formation — four muzzles, about twenty feet apart, facing north — the tails of the guns spiked down, the ammo unloaded, gun crews in place, horses picketed to the rear and ready to go.

Someone gave a signal. I was too far away to hear, and they opened fire. They fired the traditional three rounds — a dozen shells — when lo and behold they got an answer!

Apparently, Jerry had a map and could read it — and in less time than it takes to tell there were explosions taking place all around. I was scared stiff — but knew I was safer where I was than starting a bright green ambulance with a red cross in a white circle on the side. I was not about to be a target.

The French gave up fast — they hitched up those horses and hightailed out of there in jig time. Somebody smart (probably a veteran of many campaigns) decided they could find a better location for their mission. At all events, in a few minutes I was alone and all was quiet though my heartbeat was a little louder than normal — for some time. But, as I remember it, I ate a hearty meal of "monkey meat" shortly thereafter. The French called it *singe*. It was the same corned beef in cans that all armies used to eat. The American Army had some with Mexican labels that had been chasing Pancho Villa. The French had a gourmet variation with one piece of decayed carrot buried in the bottom of the can.

But the bread was good and so was the wine. And that was enough for one morning, afternoon or evening.

CHAPTER XXVI

THE FIRST ARMISTICE DAY

*O*ur division had been moving north and east — that is, toward Germany — at a great rate, and we were now in territory that had been in German hands for four years. We noticed a number of things — one very close to our hearts was that field hospitals — marked by large, whitewashed, pebbled circles with a red cross in the center — were intact. They had not been used as targets by Allied airmen. Ours had.

The dugouts were superb. Of course, the stairways faced the wrong way, so if you went down to find a comparatively luxurious underground lodging, you could be followed by a well-pointed shell. And they were still firing them — but less frequently. The decor was strictly Cincinnati — plenty of rugs, pillows, throws, etc. — what the well-dressed apartment wore in Victoria's last days.

This we didn't begrudge them — we would have done likewise. But the apple orchards were something else. Just four days before the Armistice, we crossed the Vesle and came out of the champagne country into rolling fields reminiscent of Connecticut — with plenty of fruit trees.

These had been systematically cut down with power saws (or cross-cuts) and all very recently. The sawdust was still there and for only one reason — *Schrecklichkeit* — the German philosophy of terror and beastliness. A few could have been leveled to provide a field of fire — so that advancing troops could not take cover. But this was on a big scale — and over a big area. Personally, I never forgave them.

167

Our division was still not in action when the night of November 10th found us in a farm house not many miles from Sedan — a dirty word in French history ever since the Franco-Prussian War of 1870, when the whole French Army was captured there. The occupants made us welcome but did not tell us any stories of "atrocities." Apparently they had been out of the war zone most of the time. They were hungry for chocolate and butter — but so were the Germans.

During the evening, M. Levi, our interpreter, took me to one side. He knew about my father being in some sort of wholesale business, and he had a proposition. He confided in me that the war would end soon — I thought he was nuts. He said I should write and tell my old man to buy up flashlights — and shoes — and stockings and about a hundred other scarce commodities, and we would sell them all over Europe.

I didn't do it. For one thing, my father didn't have that kind of dough, and, for another, the big shots had taken care of all those transactions long before the ink was dry at Versailles.

But to get back to the Eleventh of November. We got the news about 6 a.m. — but nothing stopped. We got in our buggies and went on duty. Nobody was hurt. We were still catching up to the advance. But the guns were still firing, and they kept it up until 10:59 a.m. and a fraction.

Then they quit. There were a few feeble shouts but no excitement. For one thing, there were no women around. In fact the day was like any other until about 7 p.m. when it got dark, and we turned on the lights in our billet. Then the old lady who was putting us up went crazy — she started running around putting up the black-out screens and dousing the lamps. "Don't believe them," she said. "I was here in 1870 and have been here ever since. They'll be back and at our throats the minute we go to bed."

She was wrong of course. They didn't come back that night, and the Armistice lasted until 1939. But then they came back with a vengeance, and I hope she didn't live to see it. She would have been about 118 years old.

CHAPTER XXVII

Mumm's Extra Dry — At A Bargain

No story of my sojourn in sunny France would be complete without a re-telling of the famous "Champagne Caper."

It all begun innocently enough — about ten days after the Armistice — roughly the 20th of November, 1918. The top brass must have concluded by that time that the agreement was going to stick — so we were moved out of the lines — and located in a place called Mourmelon-Le-Grand, obviously to distinguish it from Mourmelon-Le-Petit a few kilometers away.

This area deserves a bit of description. The two Mourmelons were the site of a series of stone barracks set in a plain without any woodlands, cultivation or civil population called the "Camp of Chalôns." This plain, roughly triangular and stretching from Rheims to Chalôns-sur-Marne and almost to Verdun, had been the site of military maneuvers from the time of Julius Caesar. No one claims he built the barracks in which we were housed. But it was certainly one of the Louis — and we were inclined to vote for Number XIV — figuring when he finished Versailles, he used the leftovers for Mourmelon. In short, the buildings were sturdy but miserable — a return to the Middle Ages — and they stank, too, because the sanitary facilities were part of the original construction.

It is only fair to add that one of our boys had picked up a collie bitch with a litter of pups and brought them in to our particular section to add a new and lively stench to the older odors. I stress the locale because it made any excursion for any reason a cause for rejoicing. Such a trip came up almost at once — the outfit needed a 50-gallon drum of oil, and a car had to go to

Rheims to fetch it.   Everybody was anxious to go, but I won, and, of course, chose a companion to help unload the empty barrel and pick up the full one.

We started off in the early morning and drove the twenty kilometers without incident. Almost at once, the famous Cathedral could be seen on the horizon. It dominates the scene from almost every approach — situated as it is on the crest of a rise with the plain on all sides. It looked like a skeleton. The towers still stood although the roof had caved in after a fire — started by a particularly heavy bombardment during the siege of nearly four years, during which the German artillery had concentrated on its destruction, but that is another story and too political for this yarn.

We found the *parc* without trouble. This was a repair center for our ambulance service housed in a building which in peace time had actually been a garage and repair shop for a fleet of trucks operated by the very famous "Veuve Cliquot" — the widow whose champagne was considered Rheims's most memorable feature after the Cathedral. As we drove into the courtyard, we could hear hammering sounds coming from what was obviously "the shop." We entered and found four cars — each was on a platform over a pit — the traditional arrangement for working on the machinery of transmission, differential, etc. But no mechanics were visible — they were all in the pits, and further examination disclosed that each one had a wrench or hammer in one hand to make appropriate noises and a bottle of champagne in the other — for obvious purposes.

After toasting each other's health, the lucky fellows explained to us that we were standing over approximately twenty million bottles of the bubbly. In fact, the whole of Rheims was built over a honeycomb of tunnels totaling over a hundred miles in length and loaded with champagne.

Again a digression. Champagne of the better brands is aged three or four years, in the bottle. It is temporarily corked, and a piece of white paper is glued to the top. The bottles are laid on their sides and the strip of paper is upright — the wine is then said to be at 12 o'clock. A year later it is turned 90 degrees, and it is now at 3 o'clock, and the process is repeated until it gets back where it started from, and it is then opened, the dregs are removed, and it is re-corked and shipped out. Of course the process can be speeded up for brands of lesser renown — but the general effect remains — a bottler of champagne has to have cellars full of aging bottles to be in business.

One more detail — these cellars begin directly below street level (why dig deeper until you need to?) so an exploding shell landing anywhere in Rheims could open a hole leading into a champagne cave. As Rheims had been a target for four years, this had happened many times, and that's why our hosts in the repair *parc* were having a champagne breakfast, as they had found just such a hole in a corner of their courtyard. Of course, the authorities had covered it over, but our gallant troops were still using it, and after giving us the drum of oil, they gave us a few quarts of wine for the boys "back at the ranch."

We departed shortly thereafter — with one idea in mind — to find a hole of our own. Rheims had been evacuated for the whole four years, and the Armistice was just ten days old, but people were drifting back, and, of course, there were hundreds of soldiers around, many of them with the same thought.

The driving in Rheims at that time was peculiar in the full sense of the term — in fact, it was unique. The architecture of Rheims consisted mainly of three- or four-story townhouses in city blocks, on a simple gridiron plan, like New York City. The fronts of these houses were heavy stone — the rears were mostly softer cement and plaster, and they had gardens in the back. As a result of the bombardment, the fronts had tumbled into the streets blocking them completely. So you had to drive through the backyards. (Many years later, on a visit to Rheims to show my bride the site of my exploits, I found that in many cases the builders of the new city had made new streets through those very backyards through which we had picked our way.)

After some wasted time, we had a bit of luck. We spotted the remains of a store with some smoke coming out of a makeshift chimney and decided to investigate. We found an abandoned, almost completely gutted grocery store, where three G.I.s were holed up — keeping warm by burning the shelves that were still on the walls in a stove that had somehow not been destroyed or stolen. They were very much at home and had obviously found their hole, which they showed us without hesitation. It was in a courtyard with most of a wall shielding it from view, and you could slide down about three or four feet and land on a pile of rubble and in a moment you were in a champagne paradise — none other than the last resting place of thousands of finished bottles of Mumm's Cordon Rouge — the *Ne plus Ultra* of the wine fanciers.

Wasting no time — it was growing dusk of a late fall evening — we filled the back of the ambulance with bottles — about six dozen as I remember it because the oil barrel took a lot of room. And we were off for Mourmelon.

On our return, we divided half the bottles with our comrades — which gave each man a quart — and then cached the balance back of the collie's bed where no one without a gas mask would ever penetrate. In the morning, we took samples and went downtown to the leading café. The sales talk was short and to the point. The *patron*, in this case *la patronne*, was a shrewd old dame with a husband in the army, and she had several thousand customers and not much to offer them except *pinard — vin ordi-naire*, which they got as a daily ration, plus the usual warm beer of Northern France. So we bargained a little and settled on six francs a quart — at the time about 75 cents — which was a lot of money. Cigarettes at the YMCA were six cents a pack duty free and no stamps. Even luxuries like *Confiture de Bar-Le-Duc* or better class *poules* were in the one- to two-dollar bracket.

Now. How to get back to Rheims? That took a much bigger selling job. We enlisted our Top Sergeant, a reasonable guy — law abiding but not a stickler for regulations — and explained that champagne was available for the asking — like picking windfalls in an apple orchard, and as Thanksgiving, that most American of holidays, was the following day, we could make it a memorable celebration. Remember "*La Guerre*" was "*Finie*" and this was only a few days later.

He agreed to look the other way while we rolled a car out of the line and started it out of earshot. Of course, we took two just to have enough capacity for the Thanksgiving Dinner and our customer. And we were six men so we could load quickly. The lineup was Greeman, Williams, Ketcham, Frank Kelly, Pennel and Charles W. "Zack" Brown — of whom more anon. We split up, three to a car, and rolled off in the late afternoon.

We drove straight to our grocery store — a trip of about an hour — but no smoke issued from the chimney. Also, the shell hole had been filled in with pieces of wood, tire chains, rocks and rubble. Nothing daunted, we removed from our buggies the picks and shovels which hung on the side, provided for such emergencies as being stuck in a ditch, and set to work to reopen our gateway to paradise.

We were visible from the street through gaps in the wall and presently attracted a couple of *poilus* and, most important, a couple of French civilians. They insisted on taking over the digging — saying that it was unseemly that American soldiers who had liberated *La Belle France* from *Les Boches* should be doing manual labor. We were willing, and in a few more minutes the hole re-appeared, and we descended into the Cave of Our Dreams. By this time it was dark, but we had flashlights, and they illuminated an endless vista of bottles piled from floor to ceiling as far as the eye could reach. With typical Yankee ingenuity, we located a stock of *paniers* — wicker baskets that held 24 bottles in compartments, like eggs, to prevent breakage. And so, with three men in the hole and three on top, we began to load our trucks.

By then it was probably 8 o'clock and pitch dark, and I was standing at the tailgate of one of the rigs, chatting with a Frenchman, when I heard a scuffle and some shouts, and a man was pressing something hard and round in my stomach and shining a light in my face and saying, "*Vous êtes pris,*" which is short for "You are under arrest."

I thought fast and talked faster — "In my back pocket are 200 francs — take them and get lost," I said. "Alas," my captor responded. "No chance. This is a police raid — my Sergeant is at the gate, and I am watched." Sure enough, in a short time three of us were handcuffed, along with two civilians and two French soldiers, and surrounded by gendarmes. We marched off — leaving the cars behind.

Some few city blocks away, we were brought into the local police station, and a desk Sergeant went through the usual formalities. We were searched and everything taken away from us — money, cigarettes and pocket knives — which were held up for scrutiny as though they were lethal weapons. In fact, the whole procedure was out of character as we were pushed around rather roughly considering that we were the Liberators, etc.

The arresting officer now made the charge — stealing champagne and attempting to transport same in two ambulances. At this the desk Sergeant bridled and said "Where is the evidence?" "But we left it in the American cars," was the answer. At this point, he asked in French — "Which of you are the drivers?" I quickly answered pointing to Ketcham and myself — as Brown — the third member of the trio, was quite unsteady, as I shall explain.

So with only one handcuff on — the other being on a gendarme — the two of us were led off to pick up the cars. Naturally, when we got there the birds had flown. Our three cohorts had heard what had happened and just stayed down in the cellar until we were marched off. The reason the gendarmes didn't go down looking for them was obvious. Only one man could descend at a time, and three men were waiting for him down below — each with a bottle to conk him on the head as he emerged. So they conveniently ignored the obvious and did their duty and nothing else, and we went back to the police station, still without any evidence.

On our second arrival, a Police Lieutenant had taken over and conducted a more thorough investigation. Having learned that I spoke French, he interrogated me first and then used me as the interpreter for the other two — who conveniently forgot whatever French they knew. This was good for our side because our three stories turned out to be identical.

We had been in Rheims on business at the repair *parc* and on our way out of town had stopped at the railroad station to use the men's room — you could have peed in a thousand bomb holes within a mile of the place. In the railroad station, a French soldier who spoke English told us that we could find this place, where we were arrested, and take a few bottles of Mumm's champagne as the Mumms were *Sales Boches* who had run off to Germany at the outbreak of war in a car full of French gold pieces — which was generally believed and had some basis in fact. We all described the soldier as of medium height with a black mustache, which applied to at least five hundred thousand *poilus*, and none of us could remember the number of his regiment.

After this recital, repeated three times, one of the arresting officers said "*Ceux-ci ne sont pas comme les autres.*" ("These boys are not like those others.") I picked it up immediately and subsequently learned that these same gendarmes had arrested the three A.W.O.L. infantrymen the day before — and the doughboys had put up a fight and sent a couple of the gendarmes to the infirmary.

Now the atmosphere cleared a little. We were given back our money and cigarettes — we were even offered a light — and they worked hard to get us to involve the two civilians, as they were more directly in the jurisdiction of the local police and could be charged with breaking and entering. But we stuck to our story and were now issued to a cell to await the morning and a military inquisitor.

The cell was fairly large. We shared it with the two *poilus* and the two civilians — who turned out to be father and son. There was a pile of straw in one corner and a pile of something much more odorous in another. We took turns standing up and sitting against the wall throughout the night. There was a window — high up — that just showed the feet and legs of passersby. We watched it closely hoping to see the familiar O.D. puttees of one of our fellows, but none appeared.

Ketcham and I were pretty worried because a certain General Pershing had issued a statement a couple of days before stressing that the war was over, but that didn't mean that it was a free-for-all. In fact he spoke very firmly concerning property rights and the crimes of theft and pillage.

But our real problem was "Zack" Brown. He was quite a few years our senior — a short, skinny, rather cranky little man with an interesting background. He was a writer of adventure stories and had roamed the South Seas looking for local color — in fact, he had enlisted in the hope of getting material to submit to the pulp magazines where he had a ready market. However, in the Belgian Campaign the local color was a little too much for him.

He began to have nightmares and woke up the whole barracks screaming "Shells — Shells — They're after me!"

He was sent away for a rest and apparently recovered because he came back to the Section — just before the Armistice — but the arrest was too much for him. He really was an innocent bystander. He had come along primarily to see the Cathedral, and now he began to get hysterical. We calmed him down to the best of our ability — explaining that with his background he would be librarian of the prison at Leavenworth in no time and could write his adventure stories from there as O. Henry had done in Texas some years before. This may have quieted Zack, but it made us even more aware of what a pickle we were in. This was the low point in our adventure. We were cold — and hungry — and our jail smelled bad. If ever we repented, it was then.

But the morning came, and we were given coffee and advised by a Captain of gendarmes that we were being turned over to the military authority — which sounded a little better to us. But first the civilian police had one more degradation for us, the *Marche Publique*. To show the returning civilians that the cops were on the job — and that they better watch their step — we were escorted on foot clear across town to the French Military Police headquarters.

It was a moving spectacle. First came two men with bicycles — then two with fixed bayonets — then the three of us, unshaven — in the clothes we had slept in and handcuffed together — then two more gallant policemen with the fixed bayonets and, finally, two more pushing bicycles. The civilians came out to see the show, and they did not applaud. We heard *"Cochons Américains. Ils sont pires que les Boches."* ("These American Pigs are worse than the Germans."). And this was ten days after the Armistice!

We finally arrived at the French Provost-Marshall's office and were properly signed for in good bureaucratic procedure and after a very short wait were brought before a very snappy Colonel with a fine display of fruit salad on his chest and an excellent command of English. Again I appointed myself the spokesman. I was wearing my ribbon of the *Croix de Guerre* which I felt would help. After a very proper salute, I advised the Colonel that there was an American authority in town that would take us off his hands — which I was sure would be his desire. He agreed immediately and sent us off with just one guard, with a rifle slung over his shoulder to march — without handcuffs — to the *parc* where the whole thing began — the repair station for the ambulance service.

The Lieutenant there, a young, good-natured Southerner, signed for us and then invited us to Thanksgiving Dinner. We had forgotten what day it was. He allowed that someone would be coming for us from our outfit, and in the meantime, we shouldn't stray off the premises. This was a high point in our Odyssey — it looked as though all we had lost was a night's sleep, and the champagne, we felt, must be back in Mourmelon.

But our joy was short lived. The Lieutenant emerged after a few minutes to say that he had read the charges against us, which had been handed to him, and that they were in duplicate — the other copy having been sent to the American Provost-Marshall at Chalôns-sur-Marne. And on this account he was obligated to send us to Paris — under armed guard — on the afternoon train. Needless to say, we did not enjoy dinner. A cloud had moved over the sun — the day grew colder, and the federal penitentiary loomed up on our horizon.

Then, like the Marines coming to save the maiden in distress, came a car bearing our own Sergeant and our noble French Lieutenant — the Marquis de Montalembert, in his very fanciest uniform and bearing the papers — the duplicates which he had personally picked up in Chalôns by his powers of persuasion and his prestige in both armies.

Now we were off the hook at last, and quick like a bunny, we were back to SSU 592 and our own Thanksgiving Dinner with plenty of the stolen champagne to wash it down. We eventually got two weeks of K.P. as our punishment for taking the ambulances for personal use — and even that was forgotten when we moved out a couple of days later.

But there was still a lot to clear up — first of all, the other three culprits with two cars about half loaded. They had hightailed out as soon as the cops and their prisoners marched out of the courtyard. They drove to the edge of town on the road to Mourmelon, and there they spent the night — hoping that we would break out and join them. By morning, it was obvious we weren't coming so they drove back and made a complete confession to our Sergeant — which was our salvation. On the way back, one of the Fords ran out of water and began to steam-up, a common occurrence, but nobody wanted to go to a farmhouse for water, so they used five quarts of vintage champagne in the radiators.

When the Sergeant heard the story, he wisely decided not to keep it to himself, and that was our second salvation. Our American Lieutenant had gone off on a furlough, and that was doubly helpful because Montalembert wasn't having any court martials in his outfit if he could help it. So he threw his weight around and saved our necks.

There is just one more footnote to the story. Nearly a year later, back in Larchmont, I had a birthday party — my twentieth — and managed to assemble a dozen of the boys from my outfit, including the Top Sergeant, who added a little tidbit to our saga. It seems that Montalembert had been transferred to an infantry command about a month before the events I have described — in fact, before the Armistice. He didn't budge, but, instead, advised his brother who was a Deputy — that is, a Congressman. The brother said he was sure he could get the order rescinded, but in the meantime he was to maintain a low profile and pretend he hadn't received the order. That is why he had to go to Chalôns and pick up those papers and destroy both copies. Otherwise he would have been on the spot himself. So much for international relations! Everyone has to save himself. *"Sauve que peut."*

We did an even split of the take from the champagne that the boys didn't drink to celebrate the first peacetimeThanksgiving.

CHAPTER XXVIII

THE ALCHEMISTS —
TURNING COPPER INTO GOLD

*Y*ou would have thought that our experience in the Champagne Cellars of Rheims would have dampened our enthusiasm for fooling with the law, but it only heightened our appetites. We left Mourmelon-Le-Grand — the not so "Grand" relic of the old French military establishment — about the first of December, just three weeks after the Armistice. By that time, it was obvious that it would stick, and we were detached from our division and put on the tail end of a list of outfits to be returned to the U.S.A. and demobilized.

But that was a long way off. The Army operated according to what is known in business circles as "lifo-filo," that is — last in, first out and first in, last out. So troops that had disembarked at Le Havre on November 10th were sent back on the same ships, a few days later. But we, who had been in France since August of 1917, did not get back until May of 1919. We didn't know all this at the time. The latrine rumors had us going to Paris — to run the prophylactic stations or to Berlin to evacuate the Kaiser's own grenadiers.

Actually, we landed in Fleury-La-Rivière, a suburb of Epernay on the Marne, at the very edge of the champagne country. The village had not been badly damaged — only the bridge over the river had been blown to deny its use to the Jerries who came within a very few miles of it during the Second Battle of the Marne. Of course, the houses were no bargain — even those that had not been shelled. They were old stone relics of a by-gone day with very little modern plumbing or other amenities.

We were quartered in the barn belonging to the most prosperous of the local burghers. He drew us deliberately, having influence with the *Major-du-Cantonment.* He saw "ambulance train" on the list of coming attractions and thought he would get men and horses — and with horses he would get manure. But, alas, he was the victim of the oldest joke of that era — our Fords pooped all day but left nothing behind them but a bad smell.

He took his revenge by rationing the amount of hay we had to sleep on. So most of us slept out. We rented rooms with beds and sheets and a stove or fireplace from peasant farmers up and down the main street and appeared in the courtyard of the manor house (ten rooms — no baths) for roll call, reveille and taps. Every few days, the Lieutenant would call us out for a formation — just to count noses. The ambulances were *en repos* and so were we.

The days and nights passed slowly — we had food and tobacco and wine and warm quarters and nothing to do. The conversation became abysmal — "Jesus it's cold," or "Jesus, it's hot," were about the most stimulating comments. So the devil found work for idle hands to do.

We had located a sister section — 593 or 594 — about fifty kilometers away at Chalôns-sur-Marne and went there to play basketball with them and shoot the breeze. In Chalôns, there was a YMCA hut, and they were selling out — preparatory to closing down. Cigarettes were six cents a pack, duty free. It's true, they said "Gift of the New York Sun" or some other big-hearted outfit on every pack. But the Y had the cockeyed idea that they should sell them and use the money to buy more cigarettes so as not to run short, in case people stopped giving them to the boys! In all fairness, there was no post exchange at the time, and the Y tried to fill the bill. All they got was a bust. The classic one-liner was a gag about a Y secretary who fell off a transport. Someone shouted, "Throw him a rope," and the onlookers yelled, "Hell no — sell him a rope!"

Anyway, there was no more restriction of two packs to a man — you could buy ten cartons if you had six dollars. And there was an Italian division near Epernay that loved American cigarettes and would pay a franc a pack — that is twenty cents or three times the cost.

By simple arithmetic, our little group figured out that we could triple our money once a week. But we had to have seed money — as it is known in a capitalist society. That's when the triumvirate was formed — John Green, Charley Williams and Teddy Greeman. Like all great conglomerates, we combined religions, skills and all the other necessary attributes. John was Irish Catholic, tough as nails, strong as a horse and brave as a lion. Charley was a WASP, cool in a crisis, deliberate and long headed. This son of David, Moses and Abraham was, and is, a dreamer — imaginative, resourceful and a gambler. So we went to work to found our fortune.

Our village was about twenty kilometers back of what had been the third line of defense only a few weeks before. The fields were still full of abandoned equipment that had outlived its usefulness. For example, there were miles of copper wire — telephone and electric light, both — which had served the various command posts that had to be linked together. Eventually, this would all be rolled up, but it was a Herculean task. Meanwhile, we decided to get the good work started.

First we snipped a couple of feet off various sizes for samples, and then Charley and I went to town. Charley was equipped with Captain's bars — our first and only investment. I was his interpreter. We went to the largest hardware store and asked for copper wire. Naturally they had none — it had been rationed for four years. But they said they wished they did have some. So we showed our samples and explained that we were a company of engineers, about to return to the U.S.A., and we had a surplus of a ton or so of wire which we would like to turn into cash for a Christmas Party — it was now about December 10th.

The owner of the store was thrilled at the possibility of being the first store in town to have wire in stock, and he made us a reasonable offer — I think, six cents a pound. We agreed readily enough, and then announced that we were some distance away and would have to "borrow" a truck, and so delivery would have to be about 3 o'clock the following morning. He started to demur at that point — he didn't want to be involved in any night work — but his wife gave him a quick nudge of the elbow and told us just where to park in the back — off the street. As often, in France and elsewhere, the Gray Mare or *Mère* was the better horse.

We went back to Fleury and ate a hearty dinner because the Lieutenant had "discovered," after some fourteen months of lousy grub, that we had a mess fund of several thousand francs. Our first attempt to augment our Army diet had been a failure. We sent our Mess Sergeant, one Fergus MacKenzie, a canny Scot, to buy some rare viands for us. He returned after six hours, roaring drunk, with a 200 lb. sack of walnuts. But that had been forgotten, and we were now really eating well. So we ate and drank and smoked and hung around until everyone was corked off, and then we quietly pushed an ambulance out of the line and waited until we were out of earshot, cranked up and took off.

There was one little drawback. It had started to snow — the first of the winter, soft and white and maybe even beautiful. But it covered the wire which ran across the fields and vineyards. We knew from experience that you couldn't just pull any wire that was sticking up. There had been plenty of booby traps right in that area — so we were slightly taken aback. On top of that, our dependable

Tin Lizzie lived up to its reputation — you could rely on it to run out of water. We had a collapsible bucket for that very purpose.

We saw a light — a farmhouse with a well head in the front yard — and stopped to fill our radiator when the farmer opened the door, and the light streaked out. What a beautiful sight met our eyes! The corps of engineers had preceded us, and in the courtyard were freshly rolled spools of lovely, rolled copper wire — all nicely wrapped for Christmas selling. With no time out for argument, we loaded the car — right down to the differential housing, and off we drove. We were in Epernay a little after midnight, made our delivery, got our money and drove back to camp. We had a little trouble getting the Ford back in place — because of the snow there were two sets of tracks, which revealed that a car had been used. We were too elated to be careful, but it was assumed we had gone for a joyride to some nearby *maison de joie* and only got a tongue lashing for it.

By noon the next day we were wide awake and ready to divide the loot. At this point Charley, our "Captain" took over.

"Boys," he said, "if we divide this dough, we will all be broke by tomorrow morning. We will drink it up or give it to some dame or lose it in a crap game. But if you let me be the treasurer, we will triple it in a week and triple it again in two weeks. Then, with a real bundle of dollars, not francs, we will go A.W.O.L. to Paris, get civvies, an apartment and three mademoiselles that will cook for us, do our laundry, keep the flat clean — and we will live like kings for a month or two and then report for duty when the outfit is ready to go back to the U.S.A."

John and I bowed our heads in agreement, and the meeting was adjourned *sine die*. But by nightfall, John was thirsty, and when John was thirsty, he got Irish, and the brogue came to the tip of his tongue, and he could charm the birds out of the trees. He started on me with the blarney.

"Now Teddy, my boy," said he, "You know that lad Charley is a fine lad and will be a big man some day — he knows how to build up a fortune and not waste it like me — a dumb turkey that will end in the gutter. But the thing is I have only one stomach, and I can just drink so much — and if we have all that dough, I will get so polluted that I will land in the Frog Bastille, and they will throw away the key. So why don't we just divvy up, and by tomorrow I will go back to borrowing the two francs for a quart of beer, but I'll be happy."

And, you know, that's what we did — and we had a great party and treated everyone in the biggest café we could find, and as I look back, I think John had the right idea — may his soul rest in peace.

Teddy and friends at Camp Stewart, just before demobilization, 1919.

P.S.

We learned on the way home that we were amateurs. In another section, a couple of wise boys sold an ambulance to a wholesale horse butcher on his assurance that he would paint it up so that its own mother wouldn't recognize it. But the cheap bastard used whitewash, and in the first rainstorm, the red cross appeared under the horse's head where it said "*Boucherie Chevaline*," and the jig was up. But I think that story is apocryphal — mine are all authentic.

CHAPTER XXIX

BON DICK

O ne of our memorable characters in SSU 592 was Alan Richard Kelly — known by his self-chosen sobriquet as "Bon Dick." This was obviously not an accidental choice. "Bon" was over six feet tall and had large hands and feet and a great beak of a nose — all allegedly signs of a similar growth in more personal parts of the human form divine. That our French friends might misunderstand and assume the adjective to be of a religious significance (as in *Le Bon Dieu*), was not likely. Kelly saw to that by word and gesture.

I must dwell for a few moments on the words. The "Bon" learned to speak and understand French in a matter of days — in St. Nazaire, where we were quartered in a staging camp with three thousand other Americans. Now if it is true that no one else could understand his French, it is equally true that he always got what he wanted while others were struggling with phrase-books.

The first demonstration of the "Bon's" linguistic prowess came on the "trip to the Front." I put it in quotes because that was what we called it, although it was really not that at all. A few days after our arrival on French soil, in August, 1917, we were followed by a shipment of Ford ambulances. These came in two parts — the chassis and the body, and we assembled them. That is a saga in itself.

We had practically no tools of any size or power — just getting the cars out of the crates was a problem. One of our most ingenious Yankees — a broth of a boy name of John Green (later, you may recall, part of my erstwhile "triumvirate" of latent capitalists) — solved it by roping each chassis as it stood on a flat-

191

bottom truck, tying the rope to an iron stake, and then starting the truck. If the rope held, the crate fell off the truck and burst open, and there was your chassis — only slightly the worse for wear. The bodies were tougher to put together. Like those cardboard toys of our youth there were tabs and holes. But the tabs were not opposite the holes in every case. So we made extra holes — with a hammer, but, as I said, that's another story.

Somehow we put them together, three hundred of them, and then, Major Barry, a fine, upstanding hard-drinking man, said, "Boys, you are not to go over thirty miles an hour. Follow me." And he set off at fifty.

Within an hour, the convoy that had been lined up in front of headquarters was spread out over fifty miles of French roads and steaming radiators, flat tires, and all the other ills to which the early cars were prone had claimed their victims — us.

It was then that our French-speaking Irishman, Private Kelly, the "Bon Dick," first came into his own. Perched precariously on the running board of his side-kick's car, he greeted one and all with the famous French salutation, "*Auvere!*" In case you are puzzled, he meant "*Au Revoir!*" which was scarcely appropriate as we were coming, not going. But it cemented the relationship with the peasantry. They threw us flowers and fruit — the latter mostly green apples that hit the cars like bullets but made us feel at home and wanted.

By nightfall we re-assembled. It took about five hours for the stragglers to get in. But Alan was one of the first to arrive. (He claimed he read the signs on the road.) And when we found him, he was surrounded by a bevy of femininity. Their ages varied from seven to seventy, but they were definitely not Marines, nor Gobs nor Privates, U.S.A.

With very little coaxing, he explained where we were (Angers), the principle industry of the city (liqueurs) and many other, lesser-known historic facts about the area and its population. When some skeptic inquired how he had acquired this knowledge (asking, in fact, whether someone there spoke English), he explained that they were exchanging these remarks in French, in which he had acquired a marvelous aptitude.

From then on he was the official interpreter involving all matters of the heart or the stomach. On arrival in any village, great or small, he would disappear for a short time and then return with the data required, such as, "There are two sisters in the second house on the right. They are about forty but well built, and they want five francs or two packs of Camels." Also, "There is a café here run by a fellow who lost an arm at Verdun, and he buys one free drink if you tell him you are coming back after supper."

Who would argue with a guy like that? Especially as it was always on the level. He got into Nancy, in Lorraine, about an hour ahead of the Section. When we pulled in, he explained that we were billeted at the place which was the high point of the German advance in 1914. He explained further, "The Frogs had only one *obi* left." (He meant *obus* — a cannon shell — not *obi* — the Japanese sash). "They waited until the Jerries were almost here, and then they shot it off, and the Jerries quit and ran."

This is, of course, a capsule version of the First Battle of the Marne. It happened in dozens of places all along the line. But how did Kelly know about it? He couldn't even say "*obus.*" Never mind. He must have fathered a whole platoon of little Frogs who grew up in time to be killed in World War II.

Skipping over nearly two years of listening to Alan and his tales, we come to Camp Lee — in Virginia, Suh — and here we are all coming to the end of our great adventure. Our first experience when we enlisted in that man's army was the "physical," and, appropriately enough, it was the last. When the medics got to Kelly, and after they had admired his physique, they told him some bad news. "Your kidneys are in terrible shape," the Chief said. "Are you a drinking man?" "Never touch a drop," was the prompt reply. "It must be that water we had to drink in the trenches with all those dead bodies around."

"Fifty-percent disability," was the verdict. It seems little enough now, but it looked good then — about $60 a month for life. They did increase it later, and I hope he drew it for a long while. He never showed up at a reunion, but one of the boys saw him selling magazines on the steps of the New York Public Library about 1924 or 5.

It should have been "*La Vie Parisienne.*"

CHAPTER XXX

THERE ARE NO GOOD COOKS

I haven't given a really well-rounded picture of "Bon Dick." I've concentrated on his linguistic pursuits, but he had many other delightful eccentricities. For example, he always drove on the left side of the road, English fashion, although we were in France. He explained this (and I quote his own words), "I can see something coming towards me and get out of the way easier than I can duck what's coming at me from the rear." If this is a little difficult to understand, you can try reading it backwards — it makes just as much sense either way.

Another interesting fact in Alan's character was his stubbornness. He had a particular side-kick — as most of us did — George Thielen, whose checkered career included a stint as a pastry cook in Waxahachie, Texas, and, allegedly, a job as cameraman for David Wark Griffith.

Their undying relationship — or at least companionship — was founded on the fact that they were almost exactly of the same height. As millions of Americans know, enlisted men (or draftees) are lined up for close order drill according to height, so the ranks marching in columns of four will look uniform when they pass in review. So Kelly and Thielen, our two tallest men, brought up the rear. I just missed leading the parade. That distinction fell to Harry Bee, our genuine Englishman, and Adrian W. Ketcham — our paint salesman from St. Louis who much later became a cook, along with George Thielen. They looked like Mutt and Jeff.

Kelly and Thielen were inseparable but not necessarily of one mind. In fact, they argued continually and were not averse to conducting their differences of opinion in public. One such discussion began with the apparently harmless statement by Kelly that he had once worked in a brass mine! George interrupted to say that he must have made a slip of the tongue — he undoubtedly meant that he had worked in a copper mine, copper being the basic component of brass, which is manufactured, not mined. (This is quite so — in case you ever wondered about it.) This little argument went on for several days. It was conducted with elaborate preambles, salutations and epithets. Thus, a sample might go as follows.

"My dear George, I was remembering last night how we carried the brass in wooden boxes to the freight cars."

"Forgive me, Alan, for doubting you. Your memory is playing you tricks. It was copper you were digging."

"No, George, you have been misled or have been drinking too much. I know brass from copper."

"If I were you, I would not accuse anyone of drinking too much, old Chum. You haven't been sober in a week."

"Maybe so. Maybe two weeks. But, drunk or sober, I don't need to be told I am wrong by a stupid, stubborn jerk."

"I thought I heard you say 'jerk.' Would you like to stand up and repeat that?"

"Jerk! — Dope! — Stupid Bastard! — What else do you want to hear?"

And then the fight was on — although it usually ended before any blows were struck. The antagonists managed to have an audience ready to intervene — which they planned on — so the argument could go on another day.

It was really never settled, and they were really never good friends, but their height and combined strength made them a team — and that's the way they began and ended.

There was one period when they did split up and meant it. Someone had found out about George's skill in cooking. So they sent him to cooks school, and he became a cook, replacing our regular incumbent, Virgil "Buck" Miller, a veteran of three enlistments, who had been as high as Sergeant once while chasing Pancho Villa but had slipped on a banana peel named John Barleycorn and was now reduced to Private Second Class, i.e., "Buck."

Buck was now second cook to George, and that didn't set well. So after a few disasters that nearly ruined our Goulash Cannon, he was out of the kitchen completely, and George now got a new assistant. As mentioned earlier, he was my side-kick and 5'6", as I was, and still am — Adrian W. Ketcham.

"Ketch" was the antithesis of George in every way — not just a few inches shorter. He was dapper and well-groomed, sported a well-trimmed mustache and had a vast fund of knowledge gained by selling paint over a large area both urban and rural. He and George had scarcely exchanged two words in nearly two years, but now became as one — like Dumas's Musketeers. Why? It's obvious — they were cooks!

There is apparently an axiom that cooking sours the disposition of the cook while souring the stomach of those he feeds. I have never known it to fail. George had been a sort of cook in civilian life, and, on occasion, if properly approached, would give a hungry man a piece of bread — or even toast. But Ketcham needed only a few days to become the perfect example of the cook — mean, vituperative and forgetful of friendships that had survived many storms.

I was included. We had traveled to Pau in the Pyrenees together and shared food, liquor and women like fraternity brothers. But now he was a cook, and when I drove in after ten hours of hauling passengers to the hospital, and it was after mess time, the kitchen was closed!

197

On that particular occasion, I took the law into my own hands
— it was one of the only times in my life I threatened violence of a
serious nature — and picked up a meat cleaver. After an exchange
of pleasantries, I walked out with a can of sardines — which I
opened with the aforesaid cleaver. But the whole scene was just a
sort of preview of what was to follow. Within a few days, a comparatively lovable, friendly member of our little group was a raving
maniac who denounced everyone who wanted to eat. His standard
invitation to meals was, "Come and get it — before we throw it to
the pigs!" — an alternative which was often acceptable.

When this happened, I thought it was pure chance. The
man had chosen the wrong vocation (he was a volunteer cook).
But later research confirms my belief. There are no good-natured
cooks. They hate their jobs, and they hate mankind. It's a blessing that T.V. dinners are taking over their place.

CHAPTER XXXI

DOPEY BENNY

I hereby submit the Saga of Dopey Benny.

First a little background music. In 1914 or '15, there was a particularly atrocious murder on the sidewalks of New York. A gambler who had been negligent in discharging his obligations was shot down in front of a Broadway hotel by a trio of hired killers. The case gained additional notoriety when it was discovered that the man behind the killing was the local police Lieutenant. He was subsequently tried, convicted and electrocuted — as were the killers.

But what gave the case national publicity was the almost fictional nicknames of the participants — embracing a wide range of ethnic origins not previously associated with crimes of violence. The trio were known to their friends (if any) as "Lefty Louie," "Gyp the Blood" and "Dopey Benny." You can be sure this last alias proved a weight that hung on many a "Benjamin" for many a year. In the case of my outfit, it was the natural, pre-ordained descriptive patronymic for our Second Sergeant — Benedict Arnold Bentien.

Benny was a fine broth of a boy of medium height. He had the build of a model for the ideal man. He was broad shouldered and narrow hipped with a fine muscular development — without the ugly look of the wrestler or acrobat. He came from that part of the Bronx which was still very rural at that time. It was called Clason's Point, and people went there for picnics. Today it is the western end of the Bronx Whitestone Bridge. The point is that although technically a New Yorker, Benny was an outdoors-type feller who knew the woods and the waters — in this case Long Island Sound.

He was a natural choice for Sergeant — not Top Sergeant, which implies a great deal of executive ability. It is well known that top-kicks run most military outfits. But the Second Sergeant is the "duty" Sergeant. It is he who announces each day who shall chop wood, clean latrines, etc. — apparently a simple task. The roll is called by the letters of the alphabet and in that order. So if you have 35 men, you start with "Algie," "Bee" and "Bacso," on the first day and keep going until you reach "Thielen," "Walker" and "Williams." Then you start all over again.

Now it is possible, even quite likely, that "Bee" is on sick call or some special assignment and has to be passed over, so it isn't all that simple. But, after a week, our Benny had fouled up the ritual beyond all recognition. When he would call out his three candidates for chopping wood to be used in the stove where our meals were cooked, he would be greeted with a hail of invectives, "You numbskull — I've been on duty three days in a row." "You horse's ass — I chopped wood all day Sunday!" etc., etc., down the whole roll call.

A few minutes would elapse, and then you would see Benny, stripped to the waist, chopping the wood into twelve inch lengths, two inches in diameter, and muttering "You guys are jerks. This is the finest exercise in the world. Millionaires pay for the privilege of chopping wood. Wait until you get in a fight. You will be sorry you didn't develop your muscles."

After this happened a few times, his name was obviously "Dopey Benny," and it stuck as long as we knew him.

He was not upset about it. He liked people and felt that having a nickname showed that they liked him. And we did — who wouldn't? After a day of wood chopping and breathing a lot of oxygen, Benny would get sleepy and often went to sleep sitting in a chair. (Never standing up — that was a lie.) On one such occasion, the chair had a back with points like pineapples at the corners, and Benny straddled it to rest his head on the back. His forehead was on one of the points, and when he awoke, there was a hole in the middle of his forehead that you could put your finger in, and several of us did. But it went away, and his brains filled the cavity. Or it may have been muscle.

Because of his rank, Benny was not a driver, and this bothered him because he had never been to "the Front." Apparently, he visualized something out of Hollywood — with a sign marked "Western Front — Be Careful" and a few men with bandaged heads holding out their hands to beg for a lift to the hospital. Anyway, a few of us — with a distorted sense of humor — took him a few miles away from the Front and stopped on a typical, poplar-lined French road with fleecy, white clouds flitting along the skyline. There was an observation balloon on the horizon, and presently a *Taube* (the German dove of war) appeared, and the clouds were interspersed with "Ack-Ack" — British slang for A.A. — that is antiaircraft shelling.

It was all miles away, but we urged Benny to put his tin helmet on and get in the ditch alongside the road — which was being used by farmers for their hay wagons and women on bicycles with the inevitable loaf of bread sticking up. It was then that Benny delivered his most poignant remark, which summed up his philosophy in a few words, "This is a great experience for a young fellow like me."

He never lived it down.

After the war, I saw Benny a great deal that first summer. In fact, we went to Oskawana Lake, and Benny introduced me to a girl that I nearly married, but that is a different story. Then in the fall I went back to N.Y.U., and Benny went to work, and several years passed as they have a habit of doing. Benny moved away from New York, and we just lost track of him.

Then one night, at about 9 o'clock, I got a phone call in Larchmont in my father's house, where I was still living, and the voice said, "This is Dopey Benny." He went on to explain that he had just come in to Grand Central Terminal and had no place to go. He said he wasn't broke but was out of touch with his family and didn't want to be robbed in a swell hotel or mugged in a cheap one. Of course, I told him to get right on the 9:55, and I met him at the station.

He told a tale until late that night — of driving trucks and working as a lumberjack all over the South and West. He had fallen foul of the law when a truck he was driving was found to be full of stolen goods. He claimed he didn't know it. Surprisingly, the authorities believed him, and he was released. And now he was ready to settle down and go to work. Eventually we went to bed, and in the morning we were joined by Charles "Windy" Williams — who lived nearby and with whom I had a date to play golf. When Charley walked in, it was obvious that he didn't recognize Benny — though they had spent two years in the same outfit. But about five years had elapsed since.

Some perverse imp prompted me to take advantage of the situation. A friend of mine that Charley had never met had promised to join us for golf. So I introduced Benny to Charley as Mr. Murray Miller of New York. Charley shook hands, murmured some polite words, and we sat down to breakfast. But Charley couldn't take his eyes off my friend. Finally, he burst out, "If I didn't know this man was Murray Miller, I would swear he was that stupid Sergeant of ours — Dopey Benny!"

That's almost the end of the story. Except that Benny went to New York, put up at the YMCA on 57th Street, and got a job as time-keeper or "straw boss" on a construction site on 23rd Street near Fifth Avenue. So when Benny phoned to tell me the good news, I rushed to see how he had "settled down."

There was the big hole in the ground and the steam shovels and the little shack at the curbside where the architects and fore-men transacted their business. And here was the time-clock and Benny. And, tied up alongside, a riding horse from Dorlan's Riding Academy on 60th Street (near the West Side Y) where Benny had rented his transportation to and from his job. At that time the subway was a nickel and a horse was two dollars a day. I think he figured to break even if he didn't eat lunch. I know his employers must have disapproved.

And that's my last memory of our Dopey friend. Still the child of Nature, even though the world had changed.

CHAPTER XXXII

Rheims Revisited
OR
The French They Are Still A Peculiar Race

*T*his is sort of an epilogue because it brings my story down to 1964 — in my album of snapshots, it is called "*Quarante-Six Ans Après*" after Dumas, who wrote a sequel to *The Three Musketeers* called *Twenty Years After*.

As I mentioned above, I first saw the Cathedral at Rheims in 1918, across the plain, coming in from Mourmelon-Le-Grand to get a drum of oil. At a distance of ten kilometers, about six and a half miles, it seemed to be untouched. But as you got closer, you could see it was a skeleton. It was on high ground to begin with, and the four years of shelling had flattened the buildings around it for several city blocks, so it really stood out.

The history of the bombardment is well known. I can skip it here. Suffice it to say that the extraordinary craftsmanship of its Thirteenth Century builders had made it virtually bullet and bomb proof. Although the interior was gutted, and the roof had fallen in, and not one statue had a head and two arms — the towers stood and most of the flying buttresses, too, which made it even more impressive than Chartres, which was never touched.

My companion and I were not given to much emotion regarding the war or the enemy. For one thing, the war was over — it was November, 1918 — about a week after the Armistice. And most of us had the attitude inspired by the British cartoonist

Bruce Bairnsfather, "If you know of a better 'ole, go to it." This is the only war you've got — don't criticize it. As to the enemy — the French name for them was "*Les Sales Boches*" — but it was rarely used with any heat. They were just dirty pigs and nothing could be done about it. Real hatred was reserved for officers who ordered attacks out of reason and politicians (statesman?) in general.

But this attempted destruction of the Cathedral reached everyone — even the blasé, nonreligious Americans, including Teddy Greeman — and the sight made a very deep and lasting impression, of which more to follow. That first day, we went in to get our oil after a long look at the "ruin" and then discovered that Rheims was also famous for champagne — which is another story — already told.

Seven years passed by, and, in 1925, I married and went to Europe on my honeymoon. My bride, Irene Levin, was originally from Hartford, Connecticut, and had graduated from N.Y.U. — my own Alma Mater. On the boat, even as we were casting off, we found ourselves standing next to two young men, both fraternity brothers of mine, one from Hartford, the other from Middletown, Connecticut. So we had the nucleus of a group with a lot in common.

Within a few hours, we were seated with a family from California, accompanied by their daughter and her college chum. So, in a short time, we were six — three couples of about the same age. We got along very well — so well that we changed our travel plans to spend an extra week with them in France.

It was during that week that I saw Rheims for the second time. We went out from Paris on the morning train — it wasn't running in 1918 — and reached the city in less than two hours. We headed right for the Cathedral. It still dominated the landscape, and we found it very impressive. It was almost all enclosed in a wooden framework of scaffolding as the reconstruction was in progress — largely financed by the Rockefellers. The street leading to the church had been renamed "Rue de Rockefeller." You could go inside a portion that was safe, and there was the inevitable counter, as in all Catholic houses of worship, where you could buy candles, holy pictures, etc.

In this case, you could also buy pictures of the building in various states of demolition and reconstruction, including the day that so many incendiary shells were fired at it that the roof — which was covered with lead — caught fire and dripped molten metal down on all the statues, creating a veritable Dante's Inferno as depicted by Gustave Doré. Everyone was impressed, to put it mildly — and I was still aggravated by this example of German *Schrecklichkeit*.

No doubt, the towers of the building had been used as an observation post when the front lines were nearby, but the systematic destruction was a definite part of the Teutonic ethic — to rule by terror. And we were yet to see its full flowering. I have mentioned that we were six in our party — and represented both sexes and various parts of the U.S.A. (The girls were from California.) I was the only one who had been there before. But everyone was of one mind, in 1925 — the object lesson was so vivid. The verdict could only be — it must never happen again!

Sarah Bernhardt's Car.

To press the lesson home, and indulge myself in a fit of nostalgia, we then hired a car and went for a tour of the battlefields. The car was a magnificent limousine — allegedly once owned by Sarah Bernhardt. The driver was a British Tommy who had found conditions tough and returned to France after the war because, he claimed, he liked the wine.

At any rate, he made a good price, after the traditional bargaining, and started us off with a reasonably accurate lecture on the *Chemin-des-Dames* — the Ladies' Way — a road that stretched just north of the city and had been hotly contested during the hostilities. This road, and the area around it for about ten miles, were part of the *Zone Rouge* — a stretch of countryside which the French post-war government had set aside for a permanent monument to what was then called "*La Grande Guerre*" — "The Great War."

Nothing had been touched. The roads had been leveled, a few shell holes filled in, and the "duds" detonated, but the landscape was barren — just a few chimneys, an occasional wall and a few stumps of trees. Here and there a ruined tank — with a big iron cross painted on its turret — was left for the amateur pho-

Visiting a German tank in the Zone Rouge (Chemin des Dames) in 1925 on our honeymoon. Irene is on the right.

tographers. But, in general, it was a lunar landscape — particularly because of the unusual terrain.

It seems that the succulent champagne grapes grow best in a shallow topsoil over a white clay base, and the shelling had neatly turned this upside down so that the infertile white, sticky clay was over everything and only a few bramble bushes had stuck up their heads. No doubt the thrifty French had chosen this site for their national monument — it stretched from Rheims to Verdun — but let us not impugn their motives — it should have been left that way forever.

Somewhere along the line our driver suggested we take a left turn — but I demurred and asked him to turn right. He was slightly taken aback — I guess he was worried that I was going into business to compete with him. But I assured him that I knew the road — and sure enough, we were on the Montagne de Rheims at the Rendezvous des Chasseurs — and I was revisiting my actual haunts of seven years before. He gladly let me take over, and we drove through Dizy, Ay, Cumières, Fleury-La-Rivière (where I lost my ambulance) and finally to Epernay where we bought drinks all around and took the train back to Paris.

In Cumières we found one woman who claimed she had rented her attic to a guy that looked like me. She had been eighteen at the time, and I didn't recognize the mole on her left shoulder blade. But what the hell! She rented the attic to somebody — and I slept in a lot of attics. Also, I was on my honeymoon!

Five years later, I did it again — my third visit to Rheims and the Cathedral. Now it was 1930, and a lot had happened at home and abroad. The Depression was well underway — and the French were not happy about it.

We were an odd group that rented a car, in Paris, to visit the battlefields again. My wife and I were accompanied by my father-in-law, who had almost suffered a nervous breakdown as a result of the business collapse. I personally was in an almost Depression-free field. I sold expensive, imported household accessories — almost but not quite objets d'art — to a clientele that were not affected by the market fluctuations. They still bought "little" wedding presents at $25 to $50 — even in Scranton, Pennsylvania, where there were breadlines, and you couldn't sell stockings at 19 cents a pair. So I could still go to Europe, albeit in tourist class, and even do a little buying to defray part of the cost of the trip.

Our fourth was another "sport." He was a bachelor, originally a friend of my father's, who had a wealthy brother. Just before the market crash, he had cabled his brother to buy various stocks at the market. His brother, who loved him dearly but questioned his acumen, at once decided to sell. So Victor, which was his name, had cash, when everyone else had RCA at 7 (down from 65) and other such treasures.

So Victor was studying French — mostly in the horizontal — and he made a perfect fourth for this quartet of serious observers of the international scene, French provincial version.

Very little had changed in Rheims and environs. Joan of Arc was back on her horse in front of the Cathedral, and a great deal of restoration had been completed. Photographs and albums of the "Martyred Cathedral" in various stages of destruction and repair were on sale in the Plaza outside the building, and, inside, another mustached, elderly female still held forth at her stand. The French call these old girls "Madame Pipi" because most of them hand out paper and towels in café lavatories — they are a special species, like blue terriers, and must be bred to their calling.

My English friend with Sarah Bernhardt's limousine was gone. In fact, the guided tour of the battlefields was not as good as it had been five years earlier. But this time we didn't need him as we were early patrons of the *Conduisez soi-même* (You-Drive-It

or Rent-a-Car) movement. And, sure enough, our tank was still
there, resting on its side with the Iron Cross on its turret — perfect for photography — we still have the snapshots. And, once
more, we descended the Mountain of Rheims — it's really only a
hill — and wended our way back to Paris, where the Americans

*Another German tank (see page 208) in 1930. Irene's father and
Victor Baer. Near Rheims.*

were just a little less welcome than before because we had deliberately had a stock market crash to spoil the tourist season.

Now we jump ahead a lot of years. Hitler and Roosevelt and
Stalin came to power, and we had a war that dwarfed the other
one. And, paradoxically, the old battlefields were battlefields
again, although Rheims was not a focal point this time around.
During this interval of over thirty years, my wife and I had two
sons, and both of them got married.

In the summer of 1964, Peter, my elder son, and Tammy, his
wife, were living in London where his firm of Madison Avenue
wordmongers had sent him to instill our British cousins with
more American mannerisms. And my younger son, Richard, and
his wife, were living in Paris while he worked at the Sorbonne on
his Ph.D. in French literature.

So it came about that Irene and I returned, once more, to the
site of our honeymoon and were joined by two sons and their

wives. And we rented a too-small Citroen and went back — guess where? To Rheims and a tour of the battlefields.

We stopped for lunch at Meaux, on the banks of the Marne, and it was a perfect lunch in a perfect setting. The bread was crusty, the cheese was mellow, and the river flowed so beautifully between its green banks that Renoir might have painted it that morning, and fifty years had left no trace of the blood that had been spilled there.

Later, we stopped at Château-Thierry, at the really quite-handsome memorial to the American Army that fought in this little village, previously known only as the birthplace of La Fontaine, the French equivalent of Aesop. So it was getting along to mid-afternoon when the familiar silhouette loomed up on the horizon, and we pointed to Rheims and its cathedral.

The city had been entirely rebuilt, and the streets were no longer familiar to me, but we found our way to the center of town — only to find that the "Rue de Rockefeller" was no more. It had reverted to tradition and was again the simple "La Rue de la Cathédrale."

This gave us the first hint of what we were to find — or not find, further on. We parked in the *Parvis* and said "*Bonjour*" to Joan on her horse and gave half an hour to an appreciation of one of the three or four finest Gothic buildings still extant. Some prefer Chartres or Orleans or Amiens — but Rheims has great beauty and such comparisons are certainly invidious.

Then we came to the souvenir stand — with its newest version of the old lady in charge. There were no postal cards of the "ruins," no booklets about the martyrdom of Rheims — but I was not to be put off easily.

"Madame," I said, "where are the pictures of the Cathedral in flames when the filthy Krauts had poured a thousand incendiary bombs on it?"

"Oh, sir," she replied. "HE (General de Gaulle) doesn't want us to sell those anymore." And "HE" was in capital letters, like "GOD." — "You see, there are many German tourists here now, and that was a long while ago and had best be forgotten."

But she had personal qualms about the line she was selling. So she leaned down and, from under the counter — like forbidden literature — she pulled out a single, yellowed newspaper page, glued to a piece of cardboard. And there was the Cathedral in flames — the ribs of the roof outlined like the skeleton of some enormous animal after a barbecue.

"Maybe he's right," she muttered. "It's not good to think about such things — for the children's sake." So we rewarded her handsomely and went on to find our battlefield.

In the square there were no more limos with signs promising a tour of the *Zone Rouge* . But there was a *Syndicat D'Initiative* — a sort of Chamber of Commerce plus Tourist Bureau that is a feature of every French city. Our search there was fruitless. Their booklets advertised only a trip to the champagne caves with *Dégustation Libre* (free tasting).

When we tried to get directions from the young girl in charge, she explained that there were no battlefields nearby because there had been no battles in the area during the war. Of course, she was referring to World War II — which was still before her time. So then we went to the Police Station, which was appropriate, as I had been an overnight guest of this prefecture in my youth, and there we found the inevitable grizzly Sergeant who said, "You can go out the East Gate and take the road toward Verdun — and about five kilometers out there's a sign that says 'Fort de la Pompelle,' and that's about all that's left."

So we did it — the sign was not a big one.

But there was a kind of overgrown parking area in which we were the only car. There was a barbed-wire fence with a gap in it and a footpath that led through weed-covered fields to a kind of mound that didn't look like a natural hill. It was, in fact, a dome — one of half a dozen that had been the concrete gun emplacements of the fort in World War I. Some of the domes were intact, others had great gaps in the side, and, finally, we came to the rear of the fort and descended into an excavation like a quarry from which we could enter these enormous caverns. They looked a lot like Roman ruins — especially the Baths of Caracalla — with the great arches half covered with grass and weeds. On the ground, there were still yards of narrow-gauge track which had carried the little carts of ammunition into the various gun emplacements. The boys were ecstatic. The girls were scared and wanted to leave. But the cameras came out, and we took pictures of the last relic of the worst, most senseless war of all.

At the Fort De La Pompelle, Verdun, in 1964.

But then we didn't know what another decade would bring, so let's not be too sure that we were right or wrong in 1917 — or 1941 — or yesterday.

P.S.

In 1965, German troops were stationed at Mourmelon-Le-Grand for joint maneuvers with the French Army.

CHAPTER XXXIII

Le Mot Juste

General MacAuliffe died recently, and his obituaries recounted his heroic defense of Bastogne at the Battle of the Bulge in World War II. Without exception, they concentrated on his reply to a German request that he surrender. It was of course, "Nuts" — which summed up so succinctly the American position in the circumstances prevailing.

Over a century before this historic confrontation, a French General had a similar experience in the later afternoon of the day of Waterloo. When almost all was lost, a body of Napoleon's finest troops was called upon to surrender. According to my history book, the General in command, Cambronne, replied, "The Old Guard dies, but it never surrenders." Actually, what he said was much nearer to the answer of our own General MacAuliffe. It was "*merde*" ("shit") and is recognized by Frenchmen ever since as "*Le Mot de Cambronne*" — just in case you don't want to say it out loud.

I have had many experiences that emphasize this Gallic penchant for the right word (*le mot juste*) and some that illustrate beautifully the Anglo-Saxon habit of saying just the opposite. As I have said, in 1925, "*après la guerre finie*" as our French "girl-friends" used to sing, I returned to Paris on my honeymoon. On a certain night, a group of us went out on the town — the *Folies Bergères* and a nightclub afterward — *Le Rat Mort* (The Dead Rat) was its attractive title.

Le Rat Mort was no better or worse than the average around the Place Pigalle (the "Pig-Alley" in Doughboy French). In a smoke-filled room, garishly lighted and decorated, there were a dozen tables, a miniature dance floor and a band — rather, an orchestra — that played the French equivalent of New Music in a continuous crescendo — probably to silence the cries of the customers who saw the prices they were charged for the "Champagne obligatoire" — a local version of cider with bubbles.

Inevitably, one of the girls had to go to the bathroom. It is significant that by 1925 she could admit it. Some years earlier, she would have burst rather than call attention to a bodily function. She left the table but returned quickly — the facilities were co-educational. The French, with their superb logic, had figured out that both sexes had the same problem and one room would be more economical than two in this high rent district.

But she still had to go, and a quick check of the personnel available resulted in my being chosen to lead her by the hand and stand by while she accomplished her mission.

As we returned a few moments later, the band had stopped so its members could mop their brows and have a drink. In the sudden silence, you could have heard a sequin drop from the costumes of the ladies of the evening who were plying their trade among the tables. At this moment, the duenna of our little coterie evidently felt that someone should say something to ease the tension.

"You know," she pronounced in pontifical tones, "there is nothing like lemon juice to take the peach stains out of linen."

Certainly, "*le mot juste*" — the right word at the right time. I rest my case.

CHAPTER XXXIV

A Greeman Found — And Lost

S hortly after "The War To End All Wars," a distant relative of my father discovered that there were still members of the "Greeman" clan in far places. Of course, they weren't "Greemans." As I stated back at the beginning, that name only goes back to an orphan boy of six named Aaron brought to the U.S.A. some time in the 60s of a previous century.

But another branch of the same tree turned up in 1921 in Antwerp, Belgium, bearing the name George Weinberg. He was the child of well-to-do parents in the diamond business — in which a large percentage of Belgian Jews were involved. He was about a year my junior, so in 1921 he was 20 to my 21. He had graduated with a degree from the local university, and now he had a job as a clerk of sorts in an international bank with an office in New York City, on Wall Street.

What more natural than that he would live with his uncle, four or five times removed? So we had someone in the spare room in our suburban home in Larchmont, and I had someone with whom to settle the problems of mankind in endless conversation.

Of course, we talked about women, but, at the particular time, I was going steady so I didn't suggest that we go to 96th Street where, according to the scuttlebutt, there was female companionship to be had for the asking — and paying.

We did get into politics and religion and, at last, after several months, George popped the question, "Teddy," he asked, "in a war between the United States and the Jews, on which side would you fight?" I never really answered. I said the question was moot and had no answer, but I didn't believe myself!

Shortly thereafter, George went back to Antwerp and the diamonds. He couldn't take working four stories below street level even though the place was thoroughly air conditioned. There were no windows, no trees, no birds singing, and the pay, though ample, was not enough for my European cousin to be shut in eight hours a day.

I did not hear from George for many years. In 1940, he fled from Belgium to France because his native land had not been sufficiently anti-Nazi to suit him. Whereas in 1914 he had been a Belgian Jew, now he was a Jewish Belgian. After all, the Kaiser was no worse than the Czar, who was part of the Triple Entente (England, France, Russia) in 1914. But Hitler was a different story, so he enlisted in some sort of a foreign legion, and the filthy French interned him!

I first learned this through H.I.A.S., the only agency at the time that was trying to help the wandering Jews. George had given my name as someone who would vouch for him if he could get a visa for the U.S.A. — the Promised Land. I did all I could, but it was too late. The French let the Germans take him, and he disappeared, like so many others — and we never heard from him again.

The whole rotten story came to mind during the August, 1991, attempted *coup* in Moscow when a young man name Ilya Krichevsky gave his life for his country — Russia, not Israel. He was a Jewish Russian, not a Russian Jew. His existence was not known to the pundits of the *New York Times*, among others. But the fighting Jew is always with us, since the Maccabees, sometime B.C.

A small coincidence — my wife's father's sister Annie married a "Krechevsky." He came to this country without a dime, started out as a peddler of toys, succeeded in establishing a flourishing wholesale toy business in New England and raised a family of three boys and a girl. Occasionally, in the interval between the wars, I drove him to Worcester from Hartford as it was my territory, too, for *tzatskis* or *regalos*. All the Krechevsky boys did well financially, and one, Bobby to me, Robert to the public, became a judge and a member of the Connecticut Legislature.

A far cry from his cousin Ilya, whose funeral drew over a hundred thousand Soviets — including a rabbi — we didn't know they had any! But so it goes, and even Pat Buchanan is surprised.

CHAPTER XXXV

EPILOGUE — 1941-1945

*I*n 1939, when Germany invaded Poland and World War II erupted, it put to an end a decade of doubt and apprehension during which most of us knew it was coming but didn't know when or where. One thing is sure — this veteran of World War I had no thought that he would ever drive an ambulance again.

I had been driving a car almost continuously in the intervening years since I said good-bye to "Kate," my ambulance, in Paris and prepared to return to the "Good Old U.S.A." To explain the quotes, "Kate" was named by our old pal, Larry Collins, because he claimed that when I got drunk and started singing sad songs, which was my wont, I reminded him of an ex-girlfriend who warbled in her cups — and the U.S.A. was "good" and "old" but not the one we remembered. In fact, it hasn't been since.

My driving since then had been strictly business. I became a traveling salesman — the French call them *commis voyageurs*, and they wear white dusters and a straw hat like butchers used to wear. Anyway, I drove all over the place before and after getting married and even after I had started to raise a family. But no ambulances. That was farthest from my thoughts.

Shortly after my return to civilian life, in 1919, I joined the American Legion in my home town of Larchmont. In fact, I was a delegate to one of the first conventions, in Rochester, New York, in 1920. And my Post was Joyce Kilmer #1 — a name to conjure up fond memories of a fellow townsman who left a lasting legacy in his poetry — these days, he is chiefly remembered for his poem "Trees." I never knew him, but I did meet his widow. We shared a cleaning woman of great abilities but uncertain dependability — a tenuous connection at best.

But the Legion bored me. It was political from the start — and not my party — and I saw no future in going to a smoker and watching a girl take her clothes off and not being able to do anything about it. So I dropped out, except for parading on Decoration Day — later Memorial Day — later still, the third or fourth Monday in May — whichever comes first.

There was an Ambulance Corps Veterans organization, but I didn't find out about it until much later, and I don't remember how. Somebody called me up, or I met an old buddy. (It's amazing that my memory is so vivid that I can see myself driving up the Montagne de Rheims from Epernay in July, 1918, and cursing the fact that I was going to be late for supper. But what happened in the 30s is mostly a kaleidoscope of trade shows and buyers and babies — our own.)

At any rate, I finally found myself in the Hotel McAlpin, in New York, and the "USAACS." The acronym is, of the course, the "United States Army Ambulance Corps Service" — a little redundancy there, but no matter. We met the third Thursday of every month — except in the middle of summer — in a private dining room on the mezzanine. We saluted the flag. We read the minutes of the last meeting and the treasurer's report — "Balance on hand $14.93." "Ah! there, Harry. How much did you pocket?" Laughter.

Then Old Business and New Business. "The Greemans have a second son, Richard. Congratulations." And so it went. But the dues were low, my office was a few blocks away, and every so often a real chum would turn up from some far-off place, and it would seem very worthwhile — although I could never sell my wife on the deal.

But after Labor Day, 1939, it began to heat up. Selective Service came along, and you had to be really blind not to see the handwriting on that wall. We had one visitor by the name of Jack Brandt at a USAACS meeting who was a retread — he had been in World War I, was either a bachelor or divorced, and went back to do it again — and again as a volunteer, in the American Field Service. He had been working out of Paris during the so-called "Phony War" — when the French sat on their butts in the "impregnable" Maginot Line for ten months after the invasion of Poland but before the invasion of France.

Jack's routine with his ambulance called for a trip to Amiens or Beauvais, always in the afternoon (he liked to sleep late), returning just in time for tea at the Café de la Paix (known to its intimates as the Café de la Pox). But one day, he came back with a different story. He had been chased half-way to Paris by a German tank — going fifty miles an hour. Now everyone knew that tanks couldn't go that fast. In fact, ambulances in 1940 couldn't do much better. But there it was. And nobody believed him until the next day, when France fell, and he and his friends who didn't like Pétain came home to spread the word.

He didn't do well. Most of us were real isolationists. By that time, in fact, when he told a woman's club in Greenwich, Connecticut, about the German tanks that went fifty miles an hour, they thought he was a Nazi! We gave him a better reception. All twelve of us. But nobody had any ideas what we could do about it.

If you have done your arithmetic, you know that I was now in my forties, and I was one of the youngest members of USAACS. So there was very little chance of getting back into the Service. A few managed it. One P.F.C. Louis Hirschkorn, of my own SSU 592, ended up as Major Hirshkorn in 1943 and was port officer in Brest from whence he had sailed in 1919 — but that was the exception. Most of us just went to the movies and hissed Hitler.

Pearl Harbor changed all that — and gave a lot of us a chance that we couldn't have imagined in our wildest dreams. Our benevolent but not too omniscient government had made a bureaucratic boo-boo. There was no draft deferment for hospital ambulance drivers. So, when the bell rang, everybody panicked — from Bellevue to Knickerbocker hospitals. Ambulances came to the scene with doctors, janitors, technicians or what-have-you driving — making them useless to administer first aid.

The Mayor of New York was "The Little Flower" of blessed memory — Fiorello La Guardia — and he saw the problem. And so did an old USAAC, Alan Corelli — and when they got together, the USAAC Emergency Corps was formed.

A few words about Alan. I knew him first as a volunteer in SSU 594 — one of our sister sections at University Heights. Though not actually a student, he had been accepted for the following fall. We shared one thing in common — he was six weeks older than I, so we were the babies of the outfit. He weighed a lot less than I did — by maybe 25 pounds — but he could pick me up and hold me over his head. And he did it — because from an early age he had been a semi-pro boxer and a weight-lifter.

After the Armistice, Alan stayed in Paris with the Knights of Columbus and worked at keeping the troops entertained. It was his outfit from which Gene Tunney, a future world heavy weight champion, emerged. Later, he joined the circus and eventually went into vaudeville with a partner and played all over the U.S.A. and Europe as Alan and Jean Corelli in "Feats of Resistance."

But when the talkies came in and vaudeville expired, he became the head of the Theater Authority, and for all the years of the Depression, Alan's office was the clearing house for "benefits," and it was Alan who saw to it that the "benefits" went to a worthy cause, not the pockets of the organizers — and the performers, who donated their services, benefited through a percentage to the Actor's Fund.

In this capacity, Alan knew everybody in show business and politics. So, when the mayor expressed his concern as to who would drive New York City's ambulances, Alan promptly replied, "There are three thousand veteran ambulance drivers from World War I all eager to do their bit."

It was not a lie. But it wasn't the whole truth and nothing but the truth. The three thousand were scattered from Portland, Maine, to Portland, Oregon, and only kept in touch at the Annual Reunion, and then only about three hundred showed up. We had *The Bulletin*, our publication, which was then a quarterly — but New York wanted ambulance drivers that night.

It got them because there were a dozen or so of us that Alan could get in that space of time. But then there had to be a better solution. So we opened the rolls to anybody that was deferred — too young, too old or in an essential industry — who was able-bodied and willing. Alan went to Governor's Island, to the top Army brass, and got permission for the Corps to wear the uniform — without insignia — and in a few days, every hospital had a crew of volunteers that did so well that when the war was over, they wanted them to stay. But that is another story.

The recruiting of the Emergency Corps was expedited by Alan's connections with show business, the press and the theatrical unions. People like Walter Winchell and Leonard Lyons told about the situation in broadcasts and columns, and great guys followed in, happy to find a way to use their skills.

I was involved almost from the beginning, but as I lived in Larchmont, I couldn't be a regular. The hours were 7:30 p.m. to 7:30 a.m.., and I had a job from 9:00 a.m. to 5:00 p.m. and lived twenty miles away. A couple of nights I changed from civvies —

Saks Fifty ($50 suit) was my standard costume — into the uniform, which now had a "reefer" collar instead of the choker of 1917. And we wore maroon ties — the color of the Medical Corps.

Some time in those next few weeks, there was a dinner in New Rochelle, the next town to Larchmont, and a lady ate too much and had a violent attack or indigestion, or a heart attack, and the New Rochelle Hospital ambulance was called. It arrived promptly with Alex Norton at the helm. He was the Superintendent of the hospital and had already put in a ten-hour day, superintending.

A guest at the dinner knew Alan Corelli, and he knew me, and so, in a few days, I became "Captain" Greeman and had a group of thirty men who were supposed to divide up into three-man crews — so there was always one on duty and two snatching a little shut-eye — from dusk until dawn, seven nights a week and all day Sunday. So we needed a minimum of 24 men, as the common cold had not been conquered, and we didn't have too many to call on. I was supposed to be the Executive Officer — not a driver. But it turned out that I drove at least twice a week because we were always short that third man.

The hospital authorities were great. We had a large room on the roof with numerous easy chairs and card tables. It had been intended as a social hall for nurses and interns, but apparently that's what they used it for, so it was closed. Now three beds were added, and we inherited it. The cafeteria was open all night, and we really had a ball.

Of course, there were nights we did nothing except wheel around a few oxygen tanks — we had become orderlies almost at once. But sometimes auto accidents on the heavily-traveled Boston Post Road would keep us going pretty steadily. When there was no emergency, we showed off a little. But we must have done a good job for nearly four years because they hated to see us go.

Like in the old days, we were a mixed bag — like the old nursery rhyme, "Rich man/Poor man," etc. Only no lawyers. New York State law forbids a lawyer to ride in an ambulance unless he is a patient. We had a couple of millionaires. In fact, the famous Tommy Manville — the asbestos millionaire who was always getting married (he did it about eight times) — gave us an ambulance — and called it one hot summer's day when two of his lady guests had sunbathed unwisely and too well. The had burned their lovely breasts, and the USAAC Emergency Corps had to administer first aid. Of course, it was not my turn to answer the call.

We lost a few along the line. One man drew cartoons for Paul Terry, our local Disney. One night he and I had a D.O.A. and rigor mortis had set in. We had to unfold him to get him on the stretcher — he had passed away sitting up. The next day, my partner resigned. He said he couldn't be funny in the morning after seeing death at night!

At the other extreme, we had a young man who was bucking for a commission in the Navy. While it was coming through, he drove an ambulance as many nights a week as I would let him. Then he was accepted and went off to the Pacific. I met him years later and hoped to hear tales of Iwo Jima, etc. He had been through them all, but he could only talk about driving the ambulance, which he felt was his most thrilling experience of World War II.

We had one call, on my night, to a gorgeous mansion where dinner was being served in a magnificent dining room. The host rose from the table, came to the front door where we stood with our stretcher, and pointed to the stairs that rose in a graceful curve to our right. "Go up to the first room on the left and you will find your patient," he said. "Be careful. She is quite old and feeble." He went back to dinner. It was his mother.

When we got to the slums, it was different. Everybody got in the act — lifting and hauling and giving advice and most times wanting to ride to the hospital with the victim. Maybe there's a lesson there.

One night my partner and I took all the curves out of North Avenue, New Rochelle. It was 2 o'clock in the morning, and the lady had made up her mind that the baby was not going to be born that night, but the baby thought differently. So the intern got in the back with the patient and held her legs together and told us to get to the hospital, pronto! Now North Avenue is wide and has long, graceful curves, but we stayed on the right when the street curved left and vice versa. So we came straight down the middle and saved a lot of ground and didn't meet anyone coming the other way. Oh, yes! We did have a siren.

One very memorable night, we drove the car to the water's edge and then went out by boat to the middle of the harbor where we boarded a British escort vessel from a convoy. She was a very small warship but had a hold big enough to sleep a dozen Jack Tars. One of them had a broken leg, and it was quite a problem to extricate him. We did it, but not before all hands partook of "Gin and It" — the precursor of the martini — Gin and Italian Vermouth, served warm.

Last but not least, one of our boys married the prettiest nurse in the hospital at a medico-martial ceremony further cementing the bonds between us. Then the war was over and New Rochelle Hospital gave us a beautiful diploma, and we had a ceremony and disbanded officially.

Some of the boys stayed on for quite awhile. But by that time I had become a lot more politically conscious, so I could see that we were keeping returning war veterans out of jobs. So after the ceremony I said "farewell" to all that.

Which I do now.

POSTSCRIPT

Lafayette, Why Were We There?

I was inducted into the U.S. Army in May of 1917 — having volunteered my services a month before — just three days after the U.S. had declared war on Germany. True, I was a noncombatant — I enlisted in the Medical Corps. But I released some Frenchman for more active duty — in the front lines — at least that was the rationale.

A few weeks later, an aide to General Pershing, our Commander-in-Chief, pronounced the historic words, "Lafayette, we are here." I have wondered many times since then, "Lafayette, why were we there?"

In the beginning, there was no problem. The Germans had become "Huns" and the one ally that was an embarrassment — Czarist Russia — was in the process even then of turning into some sort of republic so that Mr. Wilson could honestly say we were making the world "Safe For Democracy." Something went wrong along the line in that quarter, and new words like "socialism" and "communism" appeared — but the overall picture, culminating in the formation of the League of Nations, satisfied my conscience for quite a while.

I cast my first presidential vote for Warren Gamliel Harding in 1920. It was not a great choice, but his opponent was another newspaper owner from another small city in Ohio. So it was Tweedledum and Tweedledee. In 1924, I also voted for another Republican, "Cal" Coolidge, for want of anyone better. (Does anyone but a few Wall Street lawyers remember John W. Davis, the Democratic candidate?)

An epitaph for Mr. Coolidge was given to me when I had my shoes cobbled one time in Northampton, Massachusetts. The Yankee shoe repairman vouchsafed that "Cal" was the best mayor Northampton even had! Mr. Hoover, the savior of the Belgian children — he was involved in famine relief in Europe after the Armistice — and the employer of Chinese slave labor— presented no problem when he ran.

About five years after it was all over "over there," including our nonparticipation in the League, I was married and living in Greenwich Village. By that time, I had read a lot of books that had not been on my college curriculum, such as *The Merchants of Death* and other exposés of the situation that had prevailed in 1914. In fact, I began to conceal my participation in the Great War because the people I met then were so sure we had all been duped and that the wave of the future lay elsewhere — you know where, and I was pretty well convinced that they were right.

The Big Depression made it sound very likely — and the breakdown of international diplomacy heightened the belief that next time "The Yanks Were *Not* Coming."

But Mr. Hitler changed all that, and before long the veterans of W.W.I. were trying their damnedest to get into W.W.II., and I was no exception — even though I never got further than a New Rochelle Hospital ambulance.

By then Franklin Delano Roosevelt had come along, and I became a 100% Democrat. We, in our circle, all worked for F.D.R. until he dropped Henry Wallace as his running mate for 1944. Then we had our doubts. And when Wallace founded the Progressive Party our little coterie of good American peace-lovers in Larchmont went along. And when the McCarthyites of that era started red-baiting, our resolve was strengthened.

After a few meetings, lo and behold, I was a candidate for the New York State Legislature on the Wallace Progressive Party, which in New York State was called "The American Labor Party."

I never had any delusion that I would come close. The only joke was that the wife of one of our candidates said she dreaded living in Albany. A neighbor of mine said, "Of course I will vote for you. But don't you think the party has a poor name — the American *Labor* Party?" He went on to say, "Labor — that brings to mind unions. And all that sort of thing." He needn't have worried — we ran a poor third.

Two years later that was over, and the long slide began again — Korea, a few European skirmishes and, finally, Vietnam. This time, I was an early member of the loyal opposition. I knew at once that Lafayette was not there and never would be. I fought it as well as I could and still don't know who won. But my allegiance to the old-line parties was fast diminishing, and now, some fifty years later, the enlisted man of World War I is trying to make sure there is no World War III.

Maybe that's what inspired me to write about what it was like in France in 1918. If you read between the lines, maybe you will see what I mean.

APPENDIX
Chronology

*I*have never kept a diary — too busy or too lazy, I guess — but I did put down the names of all the cities, towns and villages that we visited in our year and a half on French soil, so many that the envious foot sloggers called us the T.C.F. (Touring Club de France), an early verson of the AAA.

So here is my chronology — the names make it read like a poem as the different provinces lend their native music to the list. Like Michelin's Guide, I employ the Star System.   One star, we stayed overnight — two stars, we stayed for a considerable time — and three stars mark *Les Nuits D'Amour.*

1917

April 1 —   Joined Red Cross.
May 21 —   Enlisted U.S. Army.
June 22 —   Called into Service.
Allentown, Pennsylvania**
August 7 —   Sailed aboard *S.S. San Jacinto.*
August 21 —   Arrived St. Nazaire***.
September 15-18 — Furlough for Jewish Holidays in Nantes***.
September 21-25 — Drove our ambulances (empty) to the Front
                    via Angiers*, Nogent*, Le Mans, Chartres,
                    Sandricourt**.
September 26 - October 5 — Sandricourt, to Paris by train and
                    thence by train and bus to Lunéville and
                    Baccarat.
October 6 —   Baccarat***.
Our *Postes de Secours* (first aid stations) were
                    Badonviller*
                    Herbeviller*
                    Ogeviller*
                    and Montigny*.

We also serviced Angerviller, Merviller, Vaqueville and Village Nègre, Migniville, Vexainville, Reherry and Rendezvous-des-Chasseurs, Reclonville, Hablainville and St. Martin.

Occasionally, we took special cases to Rambervillers, Raôn L'Etape, St. Clermont, Menil-Flin and Bad-Menil (not Menil-les-Bains — this is in Lorraine).

1918

January 2 — We drove, in convoy, to Nancy*** and its suburb of St. Max* via Lunéville, St. Nicholas Du Port, Rosières Salines, Dombasle and Jarville.

While in Nancy, we walked to the airfield and visited at Pont de Malzeville, Maxéville, Grand Mont and Pompey and went on 24-hour pass by train to Bar-Le-Duc*** and then *en permission* by train to Paris and thence

March 1-3 — Tours*.
Bordeaux***

March 3-9 — Pau***.

March 9-12 — Returned to the outfit via Paris***, ending up at.

March 12 - April 4 — St. Clemont**.

Here we had four *Postes de Secours* at
Benamenil*.
Domjevin*.
Manonviller*.
Thiebaumenil*.

and serviced occasionally Chaufontain, Chenevilleres-Laronxe, Gergervillers and Station Vieux Bourg. Then we drove to Roselières* where we entrained on April 5 and passed Epinal, Mirecourt, Troyes, Noisy-Le-Sec, Nogent-Sur-Seine, Vitry-Sur-Seine and Pantin to Paris and Chantilly to Creil* where we detrained April 6 and drove to

April 8 — Connate Court*.

April 9 — Grencourt*.

April 10 — Gicourt via Beauvais, Quevauvillers*, Etonvy*.

April 13-14 — With the British through Amiens, Raincheval,

Marieux to Saxton *.

April 14 - May 3 — Here we serviced Thièvres, Vignicourt, Vauchelles and Gezaincourt, Auxile-Le-Château, Halloy, Beauquesne, Beauval and Candas — stopping at Doullens*** and thence via Bougremaison, Frevint, Croisette and Humières, Blangy, Pusseauvillers, Fruges to.

May 5   Herly**.

From here we took calls to Gournay (Les Fromages), Rimeaux, Wizernes, St. Omer and Forges-Les-Eaux.

May 6 —   Overnight at Arques (La Crystaillerie) via La Nieppe, Le Meuregat and Arnere to Belgium at Ochtezeele*.

May 7 —   Cassel-Waemers Coppel, St. Sylvestre, Bruxelles-Le Petit to Remy ("Siding" in English)**.

May 12 - May 29 — Our *Postes de Secours* were at Boozeboum*.
             Reninghelst*.
             Dickiebusch*.
             Ouderdoum*
             with side trips to Waton, Herringhe,
             St. Eloy, Steenvoorde, Abeele and Buderzeele until we left for Cornhuyse* and back through Waemens Coppel and Hardipourt to Clairmarais**. Billeted Decoration Day.

May 30 —   *en repos* going to St. Omer***. Abbeville — on the coast — and Airames* en route to Milly-sur-Terrain.

June 9 —   Via Poix, Crillon, Marseilles-Le-Petit and La Chapelle.

Here we serviced Les Forges Millay, Vrocourt, Blacourt, Chapelle-aux-Pots, Ville-en-Pray, Pierrefitte and Gournay***.

June 13   We moved — via Crevecourt, Le Gallet and Breteuil — to Fransures*, Cresmaux* and Le Saulchoy Galet**.

June 15-18 — On detached service with the medics. Servicing Beauvais***, Rogy — Essertaux — Momelieres

and La Faloise (Henry married).
Also — Grandvillers — Ailly-sur-Noye —
Esmeer — Rossignol — Froissy — Le Crocq —
Allone — Gurgel-Maison — Chalsoy — Paillart
and back to Beauvais* and thence

July 14 — (Jour de la Bastille) to Trikport* via Creil-Senlis-Meaux (sur Marne).

The next day — through Le Ferté — Montmirail — Sezanne — Fête de Charmenois — Avise — Vertus to Grauves.

July 15 — Montholon*.

July 16 — Via Epernay, Dizy, Macenta, Champillon and Bellevue to La Neuville-au-Bois** on service to Caromoyeux*, Bellevue*, Ay*, Damery*.

July 31 - August 6 — Fleury La Rivière** with H.O.E. in Epernay*** and posts at La Neuville aux Lariex — Cuchery — Marfaux — Ville-en-Tardenois — Champlat — Sarcy — and Serval. Then we moved.

August 16 - August 19 — Damery**. Same *postes de secours*.

August 20 — We moved out to Le   Thoult-Trenoy.

August 20 - September 17 — *en repos* with sick calls at Sexanne*, Corbevau***, La Ville Neuve, Le Gault, Talus, La Recond and Montmirail, including a 48-hour pass — Jewish Holidays again — to Paris*** and return. Then we moved up to Vitry Le Brule*, Dempieres-sur-Marne* and Courtisol*.

September 20 — Where we worked at Auve*, St. Jean*, Perthes-les-Hurrus*, Butte-de-Tahure* through

October 8 — With calls to Sommery, Somme, Suippes-Souvain, Tilloy Bellais, Mauvre, Maison Forestirere and Le Tunnel*, Auve* (again) until

October 14 — and then

October 15-17 — to Droilly*, from which place we went *en permission* to Aix-Les-bains*** via Paris***.

October 17 - 30 — and returned to the outfit which was now at Dompierre Sur Marne* and moved

October 31 — Somme-Suippes.

November 1 — Somme-Suippes*.

238

November 2 — Somme Py.
November 4 - 6 — Blemon Farm**.
November 7 — Vaux-en-Champagne.
November 9 — Working out of Chalôns to Tourcelles
Chaumont.
November 10 — Tourteron*.
November 11 — Tourcelles* (Jour de L'Armistice) and forward.
November 12 — to Ville-sur-Retourne* with staff car — return-
ing to the Section.
November 14 -17 — at Blignicourt** and thence in convoy to
Mourmelon-Le-Grand**.
November 17 - December 10 — Billeted in the old barracks
(*Caserne Louis XVI*) with one trip to Rheims*.
November 21 — The night in jail.

1919

December 10 - February 26, 1919 — Cumierès, with trips to
Epernay*** — finally by convoy to Coulumieres and
February 27 - March 1 — Paris*** and thence by train to
Ferriere- en-Gatenois**, base camp of the Corps
— and by freight car
March 14-21 to Brest* — where we boarded the *S.S. President
Grant* (an old German boat renamed) and
returned to Newport News, Va., Camp Stewart
— and thence to Petersburg, Va., Camp Lee,
where we were demobilized and sent home to
NYC in Pullman cars — and I got in a crap game
in the smoker and won over $200 and brought it
home and put it in the bank. My first and last
winning at the crap table.

I have no idea if any of the above has any value. It's just that
the original is getting illegible, and I want the record preserved.

E.G.